Apprenticeship in Action

Teachers Write about
Read with Me

A Collection edited by
LIZ WATERLAND

THIMBLE PRESS

CONTENTS

Copyright of material quoted and reprinted in
Apprenticeship in Action
remains with its individual contributors.

ISBN 0 903355 31 0

Copyright Liz Waterland © 1989

Printed in Great Britain for
The Thimble Press
Lockwood, Station Road
South Woodchester
Stroud, Glos. GL5 5EQ
by Short Run Press, Exeter
Keyed at The Thimble Press
Typesetting by Avonset, Bath

First published 1989
Reprinted 1990

1 Introduction

Read with Me was published in 1985. It was an account of the problems I had found in teaching reading the conventional way, the influences that had persuaded me there were other ideas on the subject, and the resulting methods I had used to encourage my children's reading development. When the Thimble Press agreed to publish *Read with Me*, I thought that, with luck, we might sell five hundred copies. It was, after all, only a pamphlet and with very limited appeal at that. How many people could possibly want to hear the story of one nontraditional approach to reading development in a small school at the northernmost outpost of Cambridgeshire? In the event the first edition of *Read with Me* created enormous interest and ran to seven reprints.

This was a great puzzlement because *Read with Me* was not originally intended for publication. It began as a dissertation for an in-service B.Ed. Honours degree undertaken in 1983, a record of a year's work in reading development with my class of four-year-olds along with an assessment of the changes in teaching approach that I had made over the previous two years or so. It was personal, small-scale and isolated from any other school, apparently of interest only to myself, my school and my tutor.

The dissertation was also the product of a good deal of anxiety and many false starts; there were times when I had no idea what to do next or how to explain myself, and these problems were often created by the very isolation in which I was working. At the time, the only other teacher I knew working this way was Jill Bennett, whose *Learning to Read with Picture Books* first convinced me that it might be possible to put theory into practice in the classroom by enabling me to find the texts that would help the children learn to read. But I still had to find out how to do it by myself; the theorists – mostly American professors – were short on the practicalities.

This isolation from any other school made my work much more difficult than it might otherwise have been; it was also the reason why my final dissertation was so largely practical in content. I had to ensure academic respectability by providing a basis of theory and some conclusions (which I thought it much too soon to formulate but still . . .) but the practicalities were the focus of my work: the record-keeping, the assessment of progress, the records of individual children's development, the organization of the classroom, the quality of the books. And the practicalities persuaded me to send the typescript to the Thimble Press: if there were one or two teachers out there who had been thinking along similar lines, perhaps *Read with Me* would be a helpful follow-up to Jill Bennett's experience.

The response to the publication, as well as being over-whelming, exciting, humbling and entertaining, showed me three things.

First, I discovered what common sense could have told me all along, that there were many teachers who for years had been using what, by now, we were calling apprenticeship approaches to reading. Nothing was new. What had seemed to me, with my lack of experience, to be a totally different approach to children's learning was taken for granted by other teachers and parents. After all, *Learning to Read with Picture Books* was first published in 1979 and had obviously been based on many years' prior experience. I discovered parents of two generations ago whose children had learned to read through picture books well before school age, and some of these parents were also teachers. 'Yes, of course *my* child learned to read like that . . . I just never thought of transferring it to the classroom.' I discovered schools whose children hadn't seen a reading scheme in years because teachers who were also parents *had* thought of transferring this experience to the classroom – long before the idea had occurred to me.

Second, the number of teachers and parents who wrote to me, phoned me up, and asked me to come and talk to them, showed me how wrong I had been to assume that I was alone in my dissatisfaction and attempts to develop my teaching along less conventional lines. I should have known that many, many teachers and parents wanted more for their children than the mechanical ability to read, and were trying to find a way of ensuring that children who could read, did read. What was obvious, however, is that they too had thought themselves to be alone and had struggled with the same problems, often reaching the same solutions I had. If only, I thought, we could have pooled ideas, offered support, solved problems and shared successes with each other, we might have been able to halve the individual effort required.

These two discoveries, obvious though they seem now, explained to me why *Read with Me* aroused such interest. I had brought out into the open the concerns of many teachers and parents and also confirmed the beliefs of others. There was a third response, however, that was much less welcome. I started to find references to 'The Liz Waterland Approach' and to be asked the sort of questions ('How should we display our books?', for instance) that presumed I was the expert with all the answers and experience, that my way of displaying books was the one and only way of doing it. I had deplored reading-scheme manuals which dictated exact teaching strategies – now *Read with Me* seemed in danger of becoming just such a manual. To view it like this was to ignore the work many others had been doing long before it was published and the much better claim they had to success. It was also to assume, quite wrongly, that my school and I had solved all the problems and found all the answers. (The day that happens, I suppose, we shall all be snatched up to Elizabeth House in a golden chariot – the acme of educationalists.)

The first two responses were responsible for the third. There was a tremendous need for the pooling of support, the confirmation of attitudes and the sharing of experiences. Many teachers who visited our school said that the major benefit didn't come from observing what we were doing but from the reaffirmation of mutual concerns and philosophies. We can be very alone in our classrooms and schools, and we need each other's support, especially if we are beginning something new. Despite the wide attention given to apprenticeship approaches, many schools are isolated in their interest, perhaps owing to lack of examples or help from advisers or other schools in the area. Many teachers, too, are working alone within their schools, wanting to make changes but restrained by lack of support from colleagues or headteachers, by problems of resourcing or by sheer lack of confidence. This situation explained the success of *Read with Me*. I just happened to write something that drew these concerns into the open.

But the fact remained that it wasn't a manual laying down 'The Liz Waterland Approach', nor was I an expert to hand out advice. How, then, to share the experiences, ideas and support of people who had come to apprenticeship approaches? That question has been the starting point of this book.

As I encountered more and more teachers, so there were more and more stories and ideas to share. I heard of other ways of solving problems (and of displaying books!), stories of what children and parents had said, of books that were successful, of whole-staff initiatives, of county libraries and their support for schools, of advisers providing money and/or courses. There were funny stories, upsetting stories, inspiring stories.

There was the school to which a parent had come saying, 'I want my child to read properly, not these reading scheme books, so I brought him here.'

There was the four-year-old who dictated two books for the

(5)

book corner and, when no one chose to take them home, hid every other book but his own and then asked his friend, 'Shall I help you choose your book today?'

There was the teacher who was told by her head, 'Look, dear, I don't mind if they enjoy it or not . . . just make them read.'

There was the county that provided a term's secondment to two teachers so that they could devise an assessment and record system for schools using apprenticeship approaches to reading.

There was, in short, so much experience demanding to be shared . . .

And so *Apprenticeship in Action* is the outcome of correspondence I have had with people who contacted me after reading *Read with Me*. I met many more people through talks to parents and teachers, and they have contributed as well. I asked them to tell me about their experiences, concerns and successes in apprenticeship reading development, how they dealt with colleagues, children, parents and resourcing, what records, assessment and home contact they have developed. All but three or four responded generously, allowing me to edit (subject to their approval) their replies for inclusion in what I hope will prove an informal resource book, both for those 'just looking' at apprenticeship and for those at various stages along the way.

Since I began putting this book together, in 1987, the National Curriculum has emerged, and I have been interested to see how it supports the work of apprenticeship schools. Far from being the formal, skills-based approach which our first fears suggested, the English statutory orders require schools to develop a reading and writing programme which is based on children's experience with a wide variety of literature, which develops skills out of that experience and which expects teachers to judge and support children's progress through attainment targets that often read very much like the reading-behaviour stages in *Read with Me*.

The fact that any school using apprenticeship reading will find it very easy to fulfil the requirements of the National Curriculum is emphasized by the number of schools that have written to ask me to lead INSET days on how to assess children's progress through the key stages. They are often schools teaching conventionally at present and generally using a reading test as their sole measure of reading progress. They recognize that this will not enable them to monitor the sort of progress the English curriculum requires and have turned to a developmental approach which will match up with the attainment targets and the recording of them. The National Curriculum requires teachers to use exactly the sort of skills that contributors to the following pages are developing, and so has made their experiences even more valuable and pertinent to other schools.

None of the approaches outlined in *Apprenticeship in Action* is prescriptive. Some I support wholeheartedly, some I personally have reservations about, some contradict each other. My intention is to sample the range of thought that has gone into the work of different schools and to offer ideas that may suit your school or philosophy. Of course if you were to ask the people involved about what they are doing today, certain details might have changed and the thinking developed. Each contribution can only be a snapshot record of a moment in time.

Apprenticeship in Action begins, as we always must, with the children and the classroom, and the ways in which individual teachers have responded to books, organized rooms, recorded contacts with child and parent, solved problems and developed ideas. We look at whole-school approaches and the way staff development can be tackled, parents informed and documentation and resources organized. Special-needs children are considered also, as are county initiatives and the role of advisers or inspectors in several areas. There are examples of records, parents' booklets and assessment materials, not just to be copied but as starting points for discussion.

I must thank everyone who responded to my request for contributions to this book, many of whom took great trouble to send me documents and comments and even photographs. They have been very patient during the long time between my initial invitation and the finished book (I can only work on such a project in the long holidays if I am to retain my sanity, my family and my job; this makes for spasmodic and long-term working!) and very generous with permission to use their material.

The most delightful result of the publication of *Read with Me* has been the many, many friends I have made and the great fun I have had meeting parents, teachers and advisers in all parts of the country. *Apprenticeship in Action* is intended as much as a thank-you to them as it is a support for the many more I shall never meet. The apprenticeship model applies as much to teachers as to children: we are all learning together and from each other.

2 Schools' Approaches

There are severals ways of changing the approach to reading. Some schools have gone all out for a complete uprooting of all their old practice; others have made the change gradually. They may have begun with only one class, typically the reception class where parents, it is felt, are most sympathetic to the 'homely' approach offered by apprenticeship reading. They may have begun by moving from one or two schemes into colour coding, and then into much broader bands of coding, before abandoning the hierarchy altogether. They may have begun by using the same scheme books as before but treating them as if they were ordinary picture books and sharing the reading with the child within the framework of the scheme, with the aim of dropping the scheme as more resources became available. This last was often the case in schools with poor book provision who could not afford to replace scheme books immediately.

Reading through the variety of approaches to change, I got the impression that schools going all out for a new approach had the most difficulties *unless* they were also totally committed. In other words, if you feel nervous or uncertain of what you are doing, then gradual change, which may at first go almost unnoticed by children and parents, seems the best idea. One headteacher, who asked me not to name her, said,

I don't think our parents have noticed yet that we are tackling reading differently from three years ago. We've never told them, we've never had any comment, because we did it so slowly they never noticed!

While not necessarily advocating such sneaky tactics, I believe that only the most confident schools can make a success of the 'Dear Parents: From next Tuesday we are throwing out all our reading schemes and starting apprenticeship reading' approach, and then only with staff who have practised this method before. For most schools a more softly-softly initiative seems advisable, especially if apprenticeship is a very radical change for them and their staff.

'BOTTOM-UP' INITIATIVES

An example of this 'one step at a time' attitude is provided by a teacher who had just moved to a new school as deputy head and who had been using apprenticeship at her previous school:

I was appointed to the deputy headship from January 1988. The school does not use the apprenticeship approach to reading, nor is it committed to parental involvement. However, there has been an emphasis upon having library books at home rather than reading-scheme books, and this is a positive on which to build. I have begun by introducing Breakthrough which is being happily used throughout the school, and other changes are gradually following.

PAT CAVE

A Sheffield school which had problems caused by a split site and a lack of continuity between the infant and junior staff (a depressingly common problem) began initially with the lower infants and then encouraged the spread of apprenticeship throughout the school.

I should explain that we are a split-site school, 15 minutes' walk apart, four infant classes in one building, two top infant classes and all junior classes in another building. This situation causes many problems.

How the Approach spread
– Reception 1 middle infant teachers fully conversant with and happy in their use of 'real book' method.
– I have invited top infant, junior teachers to come and observe.
– We have spent time explaining and discussing the approach.
– Because of opposition the headteacher put together a folder including your book, various suitable publications and articles, with a note stating clearly that this was to be the reading approach and asked all members of staff to use it.
– One of our infant staff went to the 'junior' side to lead the top infant team – she is a good and enthusiastic teacher and her enthusiasm spread to the lower junior team.
– A lower junior team member then took the approach to the upper juniors.

ANN HAGGARD

One junior teacher at Anne Haggard's school describes her very first feelings.

Real books came to junior department via enthusiasm of one teacher moving from the infant department, and after the reading of the headteacher's language folder.

Brought into U.J. department by the deputy head and me; took children off Ginn books, gave them a choice – found it difficult at first to accept choice of *any* book. Spent a lot of time bringing exciting books into school – reading to them, choosing extracts, illustrations – doing book covers, reviews, drama from books etc. By Christmas children couldn't remember which 'level' they were on.

Problems:

1. Lack of books (still is).
2. Where to go with 'special needs' children.
3. Lack of phonic skills to attack new words.
4. Parents – we must have more involvement of parents in junior department.

Another 'bottom-up' movement is described by Carrie Sutcliffe. She is teaching in a school in Halifax which seems, at first sight, to be one of the 'but of course . . . ' schools ('But of course ESL and special needs children need *structure*'). We shall mention special needs later. Here is Carrie writing about her ESL children.

I am an infant coordinator in an inner ring school in Halifax, Yorkshire. The school is 98 per cent Pakistani/Bengali children, mostly Pakistani whose mother tongue is Mirpuri Punjabi but who have some understanding of Urdu and English. There are 420 children from 3–11 years. The children come into the nursery with little or no English and are quite delightful. Up to 1985 I was a teacher in the E2L service teaching English as a second language but came to this school with a new headteacher with a commitment to develop mother/father/family involvement and develop self identity of these children.

I had been aware of the lack of resources, especially books relevant to them, and had spent a great deal of time building up a knowledge and understanding and artefacts of 'their world'. This 'language and literacy' club of Frank Smith's wasn't quite as easily at their disposal as it should have been. I came to the nursery in August 1985. I worked hard at developing staff and nursery with an atmosphere of welcome and a bridge between home and school. I tried to create a love of books and literacy from the start with pictures and books they could identify with.

It was a very exciting time, the parents and children were very enthusiastic. In only twelve months you could feel their love of language and books in their play and talk. They turned naturally to books and reading in Urdu and English. The parents were interested and we began loaning books. They did all my gurus, Frank Smith and yourself, promised. It was magic.

(10)

There is still much to be done but I feel confident in my children, in the parents and in my new staff, and this will continue. In August 1987 I moved into the infants with my ideal of reading with real books. Last year's reception, who I had 'worked on' not to introduce reading schemes (some Link-up and Oxford sneaked in to the ones 'they couldn't hold back', oh dear). I encouraged language development and play and an atmosphere of real books. Almost half the infant class were rising fives. I had not discouraged reading schemes in the middle/top infants as I felt I was at that time too busy in the nursery to ask for commitment from those teachers without adequate preparation. I felt the nursery and reception were my hopes for the future.

This August the reception and middle infants areas were opened up to be one unit, reading schemes removed, I bought lots of exciting books and the new staff were introduced alongside the children to reading with real books. We started making our own books, alongside Terrace House books using Urdu and English. Soon the children were 'reading' their own choices. Brian Wildsmith's *The Island*, *Frog and Fly* and of course *Spot* are very popular. Already the children recognize that different scripts run different ways. After only 4 weeks I am very excited at the prospects.   CARRIE SUTCLIFFE

In many cases teachers feel that the job becomes more complex as children move out of reception classes. I don't think this is, in fact, true but it appears so because of the expectation that children will put away childish things as they grow older and get down to the 'real' work of independent reading. I feel that the age of the child is no indication of maturity, no more in reading than in behaviour or physical development, and that children who continue to use support do so because they need it. Anthea Purkis, who teaches in Swindon, found that in her last school this was the hardest idea to maintain as her children got older.

I have just changed back to a mixed middle and top infant class – some of whom I had as reception children two years ago. It is interesting to use this approach with older children as I am finding it harder to offer a satisfactory range of books that will be stimulating both to relatively unfluent readers (some of whom are still needing me to read most of the text) and also to independent readers. The pressure is certainly greater to 'get them reading' in the eyes of the parents at this stage than it was with reception. I think that for those children who are taking longer to reach 'independence' there is greater anxiety by the parents as they see less 'progression' than when we had a colour-coded system. It is

(11)

also harder for teachers to maintain their confidence as they need a greater understanding of what reading really is – as opposed to 'decoding'. The overall reading standard in school seems to be as good amongst the third years (who have all had this approach from year one) as it has been in the past. The general attitude to books (and the absence of a sense of failure) seems to be far more enthusiastic and there is obvious enjoyment of stories.

As I am responsible for language in our school and have developed our book policy towards this approach, I obviously feel a great deal of responsibility towards this change – I hope for the better.

We have had to produce new records to cover this approach which I feel give a better picture of the child's reading skills than just a list of books read.

We have also produced new records to cover listening, speaking, writing and handwriting skills – these may need modification as we put them into use. I have used many of the areas covered in your circular record but have produced it in a linear (upward-growing brick-wall) format. It seems to us easier to read than your circular one but this may just be due to familiarity.

I have found it most stimulating, but very time-consuming, to 'read with' the children – you really have to be convinced of the value to persist and give the right kind of experience – it's all too easy to let pressure of time spoil the sharing of a book. I have found it interesting that the children with least book experience seem to enjoy the more complex books, and being read to, while the more experienced on entry to school seem to choose a book where they can quickly recognize the pattern and therefore contribute more of the text. It has been hard to persuade both parents, and some teachers, that if a child wants to be read to and not make much contribution then that is acceptable and what he needs at that time. The amount of talking about pictures and prediction of text has paid dividends in the way the children attack a book – they scan more readily, use the picture cues and look forward and back etc.   ANTHEA PURKIS

Sometimes the courage needed to wait for the child to take over is bolstered if the teacher takes the parents fully into her confidence. They can then share worries and offer reassurance to each other and the school. Here is Pat Almond, who again worked initially with reception children and who found that the wait was well worth while.

Two years ago [September 1985] I decided to move away from reading schemes. I had just returned to school after a term's secondment (Language and Reading Development) and would be teaching a reception class. The children all came into school during

September 1985 on a part-time basis until the beginning of the summer term 1986, when they all came full-time; none of the children would be five until the summer term '86. From the beginning I decided I would have to involve parents and seek their co-operation. Parents have always been welcomed into school so when they came along for pre-school meetings I invited them to come into school with their child before the beginning of the school session. I asked them to share books with their child. Some parents (it is usually mothers who bring their children) found the situation a little uneasy at first; they had been used to leaving their child and going off before the session began. I intentionally kept out of the reading area at the beginning of the sessions to give parents time to settle down and feel at ease; also I did not want them to think I was eavesdropping on their conversations during their story time with their child.

Within a few weeks both children and parents began to feel easy about the arrangements. Many parents brought their younger children along too; they would sit down to 'read', and book handling and sharing became a welcomed start to our routine. Some younger children often did not wish to leave when school time began; no problems were caused as parents realized they could finish their 'storying' before leaving.

Parents as well as children soon discovered their own particular favourite stories. Often a story was read and re-read several times before another was chosen.

I found this 'quiet, calm time' at the beginning of the session meant the children were more receptive and had a positive approach to the learning situation; also the children were less inclined to be disruptive at the start of the session.

I have always used parental help in school with games playing, story reading to groups etc. One parent was willing to come into school to work with groups of children, especially with reading activities. She built up good relationships with the children, boosted their confidence and self-esteem and supported my approach to reading. Her own child had come into school reading, and she respected my choice of reading material for him. He soon had the confidence to choose from our class library and from books on loan from the County Library Service. Later he would come to help other readers with their choice of books, encouraging them and often giving away just enough of the plot to interest their reading appetite.

Some parents were naturally unsure of my approach to reading. They found it difficult to understand how their child would 'learn to read through reading'. I found it best to involve them with their child's reading: one father made a reading folder for each child to take a book home in.

(13)

From the beginning the children were made aware of print around them: print was at their eye level, they watched me writing labels, etc., for their paintings and drawings, and then we read them together. Often they would write their own labels which would be hung alongside mine. For a session each day we would all stop and come together for a quiet reading time when individuals were expected to respect each other. We all read – those who were only at the beginning would look at pictures in books and make up their own story. I too sat down to read – quite an eye-opener for some children who thought teachers only read books to children during story time.

We made our own storybooks, writers and illustrators being acknowledged, and our stories were always read with great pride. Children who were reading independently would co-operate with the less able children. The competitive element seemed to be eliminated as individuals came to see themselves as readers at their own level. Children began to praise each other as reading skills developed and they would encourage each other to read books of their choice.

From our reading came a different type of creative writing. I had been wondering how their writing would develop. The richness and diversity of the language used in 'real' books was transmitted into the children's writing. As spoken language became richer, so did written language.

Poetry and rhymes have always been part of my oral language work. Favourites were written onto cards for the children to read for themselves. From this I duplicated the poems we enjoyed most onto sheets which we could use for group reading activities or even for whole class reading. Beginning with, 'Happy Birthday to you', through to nursery rhymes, poems by Michael Rosen and Dennis Lee etc., we soon built up our own poetry collections which the children took home at the end of the school year.

There were times when I wondered if I was on the right track – there seemed to be little progress with independent reading for what seemed a long time. We continued reading and all at once children were reading on their own; parents told me their child was reading the newspaper and television journals. I could only heave a great sigh of relief – I knew deep down there had to be something better than flashcards etc. especially when a lot of my time with children had been spent reading and telling stories as well as poetry, singing and rhyme times.

The children all developed a love of books and quickly came to realize that reading is a value activity. When parents too saw how their child became more book orientated, they wanted to share our books we used in school – many joined the local library and would often come for advice when choosing books for presents.

Two years later I have another reception class (children on entry to school stay with the same teacher for two years). They are different, as all class groups are. My approach to reading is the same as in September '85, the children are eager to read and become readers. Some have begun to read for themselves, others are just beginning to come to want to share books. It's a very exciting time for everyone.

Approach to reading: This school year I have had the whole school year in my reception class – last time I had only children who would be five during the summer term and summer holiday. With the wide age span I have found a great difference in the level of interest and understanding as well as levels in the ability to listen for any length of time. Some of the children who were five during the autumn term have developed an interest in greater depth with stories, poetry etc. while some of the youngest children in the group need more oral work and find difficulty in sitting and listening for more than a few minutes. Thankfully during this term I have been able to use a non-class-based teacher for some of each day – she has been able to work with groups of children and has made a great contribution to the class as a whole. She has concentrated her time with the youngest children in the group with reading activities and language activities as many are reluctant to talk within the class group – some I feel have been 'put off' by some very articulate older children. I should think to a four-year-old in a class of 34 there are moments when one wonders what it is all about!   PAT ALMOND

'HALF-AND-HALF' APPROACHES

Some schools, rather than begin with the lower end of the school and work upwards, have adopted a 'half and half' policy as their way in to the apprenticeship approach. Under this policy the school may have decided to use colour coding as a basis but to let children read as they wish and with the support they want. The colour coding is used only as a reassurance, on the lines of 'Can read independently at red level', which implies that the child can also read earlier levels alone but will need help for books above that level. This seems to me to support apprenticeship reading only if the children are genuinely able to choose at any level. The temptation to steer their choice always towards the level they can 'really read' must be very strong, especially for parents. Good explanation to parents and strength of purpose in teachers are important if colour coding books is to be genuinely helpful rather than an evasion of responsibility.

One school that seems to me to have got this balancing act

right is described by Beryl Wainwright. Her staff decided to use Jill Bennett's very broad categories in *Learning to Read with Picture Books* to sort their books. These provide for only three 'levels' – First Steps, Gaining Confidence and Taking Off – and so do not create the ladder-climbing effect which smaller, more frequent level changes do. Her school also decided to go public with a whole-school approach after the initial take-off. It is, incidentally, good to see the part that activities such as Book Week and visits to the local library played in the process.

Having just seen the first group of children through their infant years using the apprenticeship approach, we are now totally committed to this way of reading (both parents and teachers). We know we have helped children to become 'readers' who enjoy books and read for pleasure.

We had a staff meeting to discuss what we felt reading books did – that is, what structure etc. – that 'real books' didn't. The answer came back loud and clear – nothing. We then decided what reading skills we need to teach with a non-reading scheme approach. Having sorted out our priorities as a staff we then needed to explain what we intended to do to the parents. We found this important. At the meeting we got:

1. Nods of approval. 'O.K., good idea, it's what we do anyway.'
2. Several don't knows, 'but we are prepared to trust you'.

Next step – We named the day and packed away all reading scheme books apart from those which we felt were a complete story in themselves. These books are still on our shelves but no one reads them. Perhaps an occasional time when parents feel they would like to see what 'level' the child has reached. They are not the child's own choice.

Real books – We issued each child with an exercise book to take home for parental comments in recording of books. These books have come to act as parent/teacher communication in which if we feel the parents need help or advice we make relevant comments and write notes of praise for the children.

We colour coded our individual class library mostly using Jill Bennett's guidelines [to be fair to Jill, we should point out that she is adamantly against colour coding of any kind; see *Learning to Read with Picture Books* page 43. *Editor*] plus our own initiative. We also did reading-age tests on some of the books, many of which came as quite a surprise. Colour coding is mostly to help us to guide the child to books he/she can cope with. There are no barriers of choice, all books are for all children at all times. We did have trouble with some parents who would not understand that it was permissible to read a book *to* a child. We have about 300 or 400 books per classroom.

We beg, borrow or steal books from any source we can. We use County Library, Village Library (pseudo tickets). We also hold a library ticket at the library in the next town.

We have found it essential that the teachers know all the books in their own library.

Other strategies we have used to help are:

1. First and foremost we have learnt to say 'come and read *with* me'. This then indicates a shared pleasure. Gone is the frustration the teacher felt when she had flogged the prescribed reading scheme words and the poor child still couldn't remember the previous page. Gone too are the children's robotic reading voices.

2. Silent Read Time – what a lot goes on during these times. A child will often say 'I read this in silent read' and then read to you a text of which he has had no previous knowledge. It has all been worked out in Silent Read.

3. Book week – great fun – visiting authors – helps children to understand about books, how they are written and produced by perfectly ordinary people. (Well nearly.) Helps them to have favourite authors.

4. We take the children to the local library as often as possible to choose their own books.

5. Parental involvement in school. We have parents in on a fairly regular basis to read with children.

6. We increased our work on mature study skills with the older children, and also increased the formal language activity work. The younger children use Breakthrough and Stott.

BERYL WAINWRIGHT

Some schools that have decided to retain a reading scheme seem to have done so because of lack of experience and confidence on the teachers' part. Sometimes this is combined with worries about parents' reactions to a more drastic change. I am dubious about calling this apprenticeship reading, since a scheme dictates so firmly what a child shall read, and how, and when, that such schools need a different title for their philosophy. They are often apprentices to apprenticeship so to speak: using a willingness to consider change to inspire a gradual learning about what that change entails in teacher learning. The comment by one teacher that 'The ignorance of the staff about how children learn is enormous so we are using familiar scheme books to enable us to discover unfamiliar areas of knowledge' probably describes the feelings of such schools. The spread of knowledge and confidence is the best support for change.

Here is Frances Collinson, whose school retains schemes at the moment but who describes the 'change of emphasis' which began in the reception classes and worked outwards. She is particularly clear about the need for gradual, thoughtful progress rather than sudden change.

In our school we have a combination approach to the teaching of reading. Up to two years ago we used a variety of reading schemes – although storybooks had also been widely used. I have always had a great interest in/love of children's storybooks and surrounded myself and my classes with material – so I was very thrilled when, two years ago, it was agreed that we should 'do something different' in the reception classes.

In fact rather than 'doing something different' it was more a change of emphasis. We still retained some reading scheme material as this was and still is used quite widely further up the school. However, in the reception classes we decided to give greater prominence to storybooks. We have 'take-home boxes' which contain duplicate copies of the 'classics amongst picture books' – the ones we really enjoy and use often. We felt it was important to have duplicate copies of the books for the youngest children as the books are in constant use, and to have the only copy of a much-requested book might be a potentially off-putting experience. We were fortunate in being able to augment our already quite extensive classroom collections with money from capitation, school fund and the PTA – we now have about 80 books in each take-home box with more than this in the classroom collections.

The children choose a book from the take-home box so that they always have a storybook in their possession to take home and to share with their families. Children change their books two or three times a week regularly or more often if they wish – sometimes with their mums as they arrive in the mornings and sometimes during the day.

We started this in the reception classes with some trepidation wondering what the response would be, and it has been marvellous. There hasn't been any wild reaction – just a gently enthusiastic response from parents and children alike. In fact now it's all rather taken for granted – except when we stop storybooks going home at the end of term and then there is great dismay all round, so we assume it is important to all concerned. Alongside all this we do still use reading schemes – mainly *One, Two, Three and Away*. Further up the school the emphasis was more upon schemes but as the first group of storybook reception children has moved on up the school the children have defined a need for storybooks – there has been a gradual change of emphasis, more thought, discussions – all of this happening naturally and not imposed.

I feel this is one of the keys to the success. It can be arrived at gently and gradually and in individual ways. It does not involve a massive outlay of money or things which may not work – it requires money to be spent on resources which can be constantly used and which should be there all the time. Books are never wasted.

Perhaps because this is the way it is in our school at the moment, I don't feel it is detrimental to have the reading schemes as well, as one important thing is that children are learning to enjoy books, to share books with adults enjoyably and to read independently.

The system is very flexible, I feel, and we still have much thinking to do about record-keeping especially and about phonics etc. – but again this is a plus as you cannot easily be lulled into a rigid routine which just ticks along and dictates the pace. You as the teacher have to work out the system and be responsive to individual needs.

It is difficult to know how 'successful' it all is – one has feelings about it being 'right' and odd incidents would tend to confirm it. There was the computer lecturer who came to demonstrate a new program, and asked the children to suggest a story and became helplessly involved with the children's enthusiasm for *Sophie and Jack* and *Special Cake* and who eventually retreated obviously perplexed and muttering 'You're in your own little world here, aren't you?' And there are the especially memorable child responses like that of the small boy who, coming from a background of limited experience, made a turbulent start to school, seeking refuge on a cupboard and then in lots of cuddles. He always loved books and stories and when at last he could be persuaded to choose a book he took it home carefully and consistently. It wasn't for ages that we knew anything of his books at home, until the teacher in charge of the special playgroup attended by one of his sisters reported that she had demanded a book to take home too. Interestingly he chose a limited repertoire – initially *Bears in the Night* (which he would 'read' as a fairly accurate list of prepositions) alternated with *Funnybones*, which was 'read' as 'dark dark' on every page interspersed with lots of chuckles. The book choice has widened very gradually during the year and he even commented one day 'I'll have a new book' when he took *Mr Gumpy's Outing* for the first time.

I should also mention that I am fortunate to have a band of mother helpers who have willingly sat often smothered in children immersed in storybooks.

We have been and still are fascinated to be involved in the reactions to books – the 'fashions' which change during the year and from year to year, the responses of children and parents.

I'm fortunate that I love books and I think it is very important in this approach to become involved in books – one has to be actively involved. I'm still staggered to think that children are denied access to books (kept tidily on high shelves) but it is essential to be sympathetic and sensitive, not to rush in and impose, on parents or other members of staff – it has to be natural and sincere. At the same time teachers, parents, and children can be helped into book involvement – it can so easily take off from storytime, which is a basic child activity. People should be encouraged to try it and see – perhaps to start from storytimes: to think about books and stories, talk with children, basing classroom activities on stories (we have made some toys from our favourites – Rosie the Hen, Sophie and Jack) and making books more freely available, and then hopefully things will take off quite naturally. There is no better way of encouraging teachers and parents into a greater children's book awareness than by sharing books regularly with children.

FRANCES COLLINSON

Breakthrough also provides a support to the development of some less formal approaches, since there is no prescribed vocabulary or method of working. In the following report Breakthrough is combined with 'real books' *and* the reading scheme – which seems a real case of belt and braces! Interestingly, the approach in this school *began* with children with special needs.

Any curriculum change does not happen overnight and can cause disagreement and uncertainty among fellow professionals. Introducing a 'revolutionary' approach which challenged the school's traditional ways of thinking was, therefore, both exciting and frustrating.

For two terms I used the apprenticeship approach within my reception class – to encourage children who had little interest in books and those with severe language difficulties, at first. It very soon became a supplement to the reading scheme, involving the whole class.

However, even with two carefully selected mums, I was desperately short of 'masters'. (At this stage books were not going home and parents were not involved.) Cross-age peer tutoring seemed to be the answer.

With the co-operation of the special needs teacher, who had also been using this approach, and a sympathetic colleague in the junior department, a rota of 3rd year children was arranged. Ben (fully conversant with the method through special needs) passed on his expertise to fellow pupils, who spent twenty minutes each morning in my classroom. An interesting spin-off occurred. Ben's confidence grew; his work improved and his attitude to school became much more positive.

Eventually I was able to present a case to my head for the

introduction of this approach into the infant curriculum.

After an informal parents' evening (support was overwhelming) and with the help of the Library Service, we were in business.

The reading scheme is still in use, and I have had to compromise to a certain extent. However, I now use storybooks alongside Breakthrough, which has been updated, with Ginn 360 slotted in. Using level one discussion books with a group of children, who then take the same book home to read with mum or dad, works well. As there is no pressure to learn all the words before we go on to the next book, no child fails to progress.

Because the children are now used to re-reading favourites, I can present level 2 as a fun activity each week. With some children it's 'Do you remember when Ben . . . ', with others it's 'Let's see what happens to Ben and Lad next . . . ', depending on their confidence. In this way, they progress through the schemes as required but at their own pace and with the minimum of pressure. Plenty of support is given with each new book.

I find that children will often choose to take a reading scheme book home, sometimes going back to level one.

In all other respects reception and middle infants use the approach as described in *Read with Me*. Although she does use Breakthrough, our top infant teacher remains unconvinced and it would be wrong to impose this approach upon her. As we have discovered, reading together cannot be practised half-heartedly; a great deal of commitment is required.

Finding time during the day to change books has proved difficult. Perhaps the answer would be to let children choose books with mum before or after school.

To the children and adults involved, however, this has been an enlightening and stimulating year. We still have areas to refine – record-keeping, follow-up sessions for parents, more parental help within the classroom. I can see a change taking place and the reading scheme being phased out, but it is a slow and sometimes painful process.

As a reception teacher, I find this approach exciting and challenging. It has made me think seriously about my attitude towards other areas of the curriculum. However, as professionals we must respect the right of others to disagree with us.

MARY FOSSEY

One teacher who is working in some degree of isolation in her school also feels the need to continue the scheme so that her children are not at a disadvantage and also so that she is not defying the school policy within which she must still work.

I am at a school where apprenticeship reading is run alongside scheme readers. Previously I taught in a school whose head preferred scheme readers but I was delighted to see the response to discussion of books read throughout the day from my 'on the carpet box'. Book reviews emerged (written and pictorial) from much discussion, and of course several children poring over a book together was not uncommon. I had two non-readers who were on a special needs scheme and were not supposed to read other books. With the head's approval (desperation?) I showed these two some pre-Ginn readers. When they came to me to read while the rest of the class was sitting reading quietly around us, I realized one day that nearly all the children were listening to me and those near to us craning their necks to see the pictures. After that we often shared the books and when my two late readers were praised particularly highly by me there were encouraging grins and sometimes clapping for them − we all shared their triumphs.

On coming to my present school I was thrilled to see the 'home reader' comment books which go home each night for parents to write in. I do feel there is some ignorance of what apprenticeship reading is all about. I got such comments as 'this book is too easy', 'he has had this twice already', 'is this a reading book?' (about a Ladybird Interest book) and enquiries at parents' evening as to where he/she was in reading? I feel the reason for this use of scheme readers as well is a 'hedging of bets' because of the pressure from middle-class, academically minded parents. And also because of some staff being uncommitted or opposed to apprenticeship reading.

Some staff spend a lot of time in hearing the scheme readers; one has abandoned the 'real reading' completely. I have been asked to pay 'lip service' to the school scheme readers till we find out how the new head feels. I spend a lot of time discussing books, sharing them and reading with the children individually. (Once a week I hear schemes which, I feel, is a farce as most of the children are uninterested and could 'romp' through the book if allowed to.) I now, having had this infant class last term (we are now 1st year juniors), have a better understanding of the individual needs of each child and its parents, and I am beginning some superb 'conversations' with a few parents by way of the comment books.

I do have my reservations about apprenticeship reading for the odd child and also have not fully sorted out how one gauges a child's progress for yearly reports etc. Should one have a termly/yearly reading age test? If so − what does it reflect and is it really necessary and indicative of the achievements of the approach? These are 'niggles' as I am still very excited by 'real reading' as I like to call it. As it seems to me we are educating children for life-long reading, not to jump through hoops and then turn away from books once they leave school.   JILL DUCKETT

Jill Duckett raises the question of reading-age tests. It's worth noting that requirements for assessment of reading progress under the National Curriculum do not include formal reading-age testing, a point which will be picked up later.

Finally, in this group of 'half-and-half' approaches, is Barbara Payne's class. She initially retained scheme books because of lack of resources but is now refining her collection so that the only books offered are those the children like, regardless of origin.

I started the apprenticeship approach last September with a complete class (22) of new entrants, all first years with birthdays between September and April. We have a high proportion of children with learning problems, disruptive behaviour etc.

I felt as though I had jumped into very deep waters to begin with but found that the children accepted and enjoyed this approach so much that I could relax and accept pointers to the next step forward from them.

Initially, there was not a wide choice of books, but I built up the classroom library gradually so that at this end of the year there is a very wide choice. There are also other books available (reference books, topic books and more fiction) which I read to them and which they can look at anytime but we do not read these together yet.

You ask about the influence of individual books on children. The range is very wide and it is often possible to see the reasons for the child's choice.

The Story Chest 'Little Pig' was a breakthrough for at least three children in February. This followed a dramatic presentation of 'Three Little Pigs' for assembly at the end of January. Other notable quirks are the boy who often chooses a story that no one else has read, the boy who obviously chooses for subject interest and two of the best readers who are only just being persuaded not to choose the very easiest books every time. It does seem as though the less mature children choose for sound rather than meaning, i.e. nursery rhymes, *The Jigaree* and *Hairy Bear*, whereas the more advanced ones are influenced by subject matter as well.

Compared to the flash card and reading scheme system, with which I have worked up to now, this approach opens up a vast range of language and experiences to the children. They all get equal attention and satisfaction from their story sessions. Their expectations of the spoken and written word are more sophisticated and listening skills improve. Also there is the opportunity to build up a warmer relationship between child and teacher and between the class as a whole, in sharing books we have all enjoyed.

Two splendid mothers have been helping me through the year

on a regular basis and each child gets three sessions a week. Time (or lack of it) is the biggest problem – on my own I could not have managed. Also, with insecure, disruptive children any reading session is open to constant interruptions.   BARBARA PAYNE

WHOLE-SCHOOL APPROACHES

So far in this chapter, I have looked at schools that have started apprenticeship in a limited way, either through a bottom-up approach, as I did, or through a half-and-half approach. Both provide support while the school and the parents are feeling their way into a new system and are observing and learning about the children's progress. Some schools, however, decide to make a whole-school commitment from the start. This is harder to do and there are often pitfalls that cannot be foreseen in advance. One school decided to adopt a whole-school policy on the arrival of a new headteacher. (Like many schools that choose to change immediately and completely, Christian Malford is a small village school in which consensus can, presumably, be more easily reached!)

I came to Christian Malford School as headteacher in April 1985, taking over the top class consisting of 2nd, 3rd and 4th year juniors – no reading scheme books in the class. Kathryn had been appointed one term earlier to take over the first class of lower, middle and top infants.

It became apparent fairly quickly that Kathryn and I were like-minded in terms of our feelings about reading scheme books and consequently, having given Kathryn the apprenticeship booklet to read, we decided to work that way from the following September.

The great mistake we made at this stage was not involving parents. Our second mistake was our timing. Kathryn was out on a course for a six-week block from mid-October to mid-November and so we had a supply teacher in at the point when the approach was just getting under way. Needless to say, eyebrows were raised and questions asked. All very justifiable and what I should have anticipated.

As a consequence of the questioning by parents we held a meeting in February of the following term (1986). We in fact feel now that this is the term when we really started. The response to the meeting was fairly good, but over the succeeding 18 months there were still one or two parents who questioned and worried. The apparent lack of structure, of course, does not enable them to 'measure progress' in the traditional way.

We feel standards of reading in the infants are at least as good,

CHRISTIAN MALFORD PRIMARY SCHOOL

Suggested strategies for developing Apprenticeship Reading

The following strategies have arisen from staff discussions on developing the Apprenticeship Reading approach throughout the school. They are by no means exhaustive and obviously reflect our personal thinking. They have arisen from our firm belief in the ACTIVE role of the teacher in the Apprenticeship approach to reading.

1. The Environment

   1.1) Ensure the book area is secure and attractive for the child.
   1.2) Make sure books are well displayed.
   1.3) Encourage children to tidy and care for the books.
   1.4) Try to have as large a selection of books as possible (a difficult one this!).
   1.5) Make the book corner a special place.

2. Classroom Activities

   2.1) Spend book time with children individually, reading to child, holding book with child, sharing and enjoying book together.
   2.2) Re-inforce directionality when sharing books (running finger along line, or letting child do same).
   2.3) Monitor child's choice of books in order to encourage them to diversify without destroying enthusiasm or confidence.
   2.4) When sharing a book teacher may:-
        read aloud to child
        read aloud with child
        listen to child read aloud
   2.5) Develop work on phonics (especially initial blends) to help children identify words in context. Breakthrough to Literacy and word banks help in this area.
   2.6) Keep records of child's reading behaviour.
   2.7) Develop a method of recording books read which the children can carry out for themselves (e.g., `book of the of week' for beginning readers, leading to all books for older children).
   2.8) Carry out book related activities - painting. drawing, acting, book reviews, etc.
   2.9) All children should have a quiet book time each day leading to U.S.S.R. (Uninterrupted, Sustained, Silent Reading).
   2.10) Talk to children about how to choose books (an important skill), including the use of the 5-finger exercise: Child scans first page of book, puts down one finger for each word spotted that s/he can't read. Five fingers down, book is probably too hard. Child can do this quite privately.

3. Teacher Attitude

   3.1) Always re-inforce success making every child feel s/he is a reader.
   3.2) Allow child time to prepare before sharing a book.
   3.3) Use words `read with me' or `share a book with me'.
   3.4) Supporting the child in his/her reading is vital, by helping with or supplying unknown words.
   3.5) Encourage parental support, under teacher guidance.
   3.6) Be enthusiastic about books, talking, sharing and reading to class regularly.
   3.7) Allow children time to browse, etc., to talk to and share books with one another.
   3.8) It is crucially important to get the message across that reading is obtaining meaning from print.
   3.9) Above all encourage enthusiasm and enjoyment and use lots of PRAISE!

if not better than they were, but as we don't test infants we can't prove it with figures! The love of books is apparent everywhere – the only problem is that we can't get enough of them!

JAN MAXWELL

The infant teacher at Christian Malford describes her personal view of the process. You will remember my suggestion that a complete changeover is most successful when the staff are knowledgeable and fully committed already. This school seems to me the perfect example of this, enabling them to succeed even in the face of a miscalculation over parental contact.

When I first started the 'Apprenticeship Approach' to reading there were 25 children in the class. Some (the majority) of the children had been reading *One, Two, Three and Away* since they had been coming to school (two years in some cases). There were still children who thought they couldn't read, because they were *only on book* . . . and some of them took a lot of convincing that they could read because they knew names and signs.

To introduce the approach to the children I suggested that there were lots of different books in the classroom, and the school, which we didn't look at very often. Perhaps they'd like to look at and read some of them. Could they find a favourite book? We shared these books, found out what we liked about them. Shared them with a friend and then talked about them.

I no longer asked the children to 'read to me' but asked them to 'share a book with me'. I would sit on the floor with them and they would cuddle up. The atmosphere was very relaxed, with some exceptions: these were the children whose parents were appearing to put the pressure on. Asking them to take home 'the next one' of *One, Two, Three and Away*. One of this group of about five children used to sweat profusely when reading; he wouldn't guess at words or look at initial letters. There was a very great fear in him. I suggested that he chose books other than *One, Two, Three and Away* and he began to choose 'Story Chest' books to read to me but continued to take home *One, Two, Three and Away*. Things did relax but he continued to think he couldn't read for quite a long time. He is now 'a reader'.

To begin with the children chose books well below the level that they could have coped with, but they were finding their feet.

There were problems in continuity when I was away for several weeks, which did hinder the progress, and also didn't help the understanding of the system with parents, as Jan mentioned.

The children quickly fell into the pattern of choosing books for themselves at appropriate levels. There were, and still are, occasions when the children choose books 'too difficult' or 'too easy' but there is often an explanation for this.

When the new children arrived in the class after Christmas (1986), the other children were very eager to 'share' books with them. (This has continued.) This encouraged me, as their eagerness for books had definitely changed from 'oh no not reading' to a real enjoyment of books. Especially when one new child said to an established child, 'I can't read', and the reply was, 'You can, everyone can read'. Now at the beginning of the third year of this approach there has been no one who would say they couldn't read.

There are still children who have difficulty with reading, but they don't see themselves as failures, which they appeared to do previously. The children enjoy books and the more they are given a variety of books and encouraged the more confident they become.

The other plus is that the children don't realize that they have learnt to read. There have been one or two instances when children have come to me and said, not that they can't read but when are they going to learn to read. They do need convincing, so I choose a book which I know they haven't seen before, and ask them to share it with me. Then they realize that they can read.

When the new children come in they share the books just by looking at the pictures and telling me what they think the story is, and also by me reading the book to them, and looking at the pictures and asking them to guess what will happen next.

One of the next main stages (because there seem to me to be as many stages as children, and you have to know the children to discover what is best to do next with them), is when they recite a story e.g. a nursery rhyme. Then with other books they will pretend to read the story.

Next I try and get them to put their fingers under the words as they read 'with me'. Then there is the time when I miss words and they say them. There is also the time when they 'know the book' and 'read it', and when they 'know the book' and I can tell by watching their eyes and fingers that they really can read the book.

KATHRYN NICHOLAS

A Doncaster school emphasizes the need, in these circumstances especially, to make parents part of the process at the very beginning. If your change is going to be public, it must be explained. Parents will be involved in the reading process so they must understand what you mean by reading and how you want them to help. You, in turn, must be absolutely sure what you mean when you are talking or writing to parents. Which is why I said at the beginning of this chapter that the whole-school changeover is the one least likely to succeed, unless the teachers are both knowledgeable and confident. It is not, I feel, the best

(27)

approach for teachers who are unsure of themselves, the books or their children. Where it is successful, however, the rewards are great.

During the last year we have adopted the Apprenticeship Approach to reading which I discovered after reading an article in the *Times Ed.* 5.7.85. It made me think, this is what one does naturally with one's own children, but never thought to extend it into the classroom.

This led to a research study (within a Diploma in Children's Literature) 'Do Young Children Prefer Real Books or Reading Scheme Books?': the outcome was obvious. I introduced your booklet to my head – and it snowballed into a school policy.

I really feel I can only reiterate the points you have made in *Read with Me*. I would not change back to other approaches to reading. I am convinced this is the way, and wonder why I didn't use it before.

I feel it is important to let parents know what is happening, to invite them into the classroom and show them. I feel it is also important to appreciate and give parents credit for all the work they do with their children, to show we value them.

I feel an enormous benefit the children have from the Apprenticeship Approach is the language experience they gain. The group/class discussions, sharing books with a variety of adults, each bringing an individual language experience to the listener in the early stages, benefits later sharing.

An example of this is Rebecca's story (age five – reception year). 'Once upon a time there was a princess who lived in a castle. One day the princess ran away and got lost in a dark, dark wood. The princess looked for her way back home and couldn't find it so a wizard snapped his fingers and then she was home.'

I found the children were 'reading' with understanding and enjoyment, and the emotional response was fantastic. This was extended into play. Steven, a very very quiet boy, came to life as a 'wicked witch'.

I found children who had no formal phonetic teaching were building words naturally and tackling unknown text confidently.

I did have moments of panic but re-read your booklet and felt reassured. It was around the stage that children were tackling unknown text. The right material appeared to be extremely important to reading behaviour at this stage. You have to know the books available very well and match them to the individual. Also it needs stressing to all that reading does slow down to a word-by-word rate; also that knowing when a child has reached this stage is important.   JANE RICHARDS

It is often noticeable that where the changeover has been most successful, teachers describe what is almost a 'literary immersion' technique: not only reading stories to and with children but using wall stories, library visits, big books, silent reading, book weeks, and peer-group reading. Carole Mander's Royston school is one such.

We have been aware of the shared approach to reading for some time. Following INSET activities at the Teachers' Centre, staff involvement in studying theory, and visiting other schools, we held a full afternoon's meeting to plan the organization, management and implementation of this approach. The conclusion was that children would gain in confidence and enjoyment in choosing their own books and reading whole stories with meaning, fun and purpose.

We have noticed a more confident approach to choosing books. Children read believing themselves to be 'readers' without the competitive element. Those who began in the nursery class have gained a positive attitude and success.

We have had changes of staff (and in a small school that can be traumatic) who have willingly adjusted to this approach.

We introduced the idea with a parents' evening when Rosemary Stubbs and Chris Davis came to validate my statements. We made a video of *our* children actively being involved with their books. Then we had a small group discussion time (95 per cent turn out). Parents have been extremely supportive, many come in to help in the classroom. The results of those children whose parents have been involved have been extremely exciting.

We have 'Story Chest' books throughout the ages. In addition we have a wide variety of storybooks from other 'schemes' to the Schools Library Service's. We have picture books to classics. There are three classes – nursery, infant and 1st/2nd year junior. Each room has boxes of books which have been carefully chosen to relate 'generally' to the average ability range within the class.

We also have picture books in each room and 'easier-harder' books in each selection. Books are regularly exchanged with Schools Library Service. I am constantly updating, renewing and adding to the books.

Children get together as classes and share favourites, suggest books which others would like, leave books which have been discussed in other rooms. Juniors keep a short record of their books: author – publisher – title and brief comment at end. This enables so much more discussion on artistic content, language, knowledge of authors and their styles, publishers.

They have to be restricted in discussion times because they now read prolifically and have a large pile in a short time to share.

We use the Stubbs/Davis profiles and your wheel. We also keep written records of the books read by each child. We have devised a small booklet to liaise with home and school. CAROLE MANDER

Not all schools moving to apprenticeship as a unified policy are small ones. Two large primaries have been developing their reading programmes along these lines for several years. I've visited them both, and the enthusiasm, knowledge and commitment of the heads and staff were obviously the clue to their success. The language policy document of Waterbeach Community Primary School emphasizes the whole-school approach in its note that 'reading is the responsibility of ALL teachers of children of primary age. It is a process which is as important in the juniors as in the infants. It is also the responsibility of all teachers to be thoroughly familiar with the processes used throughout the school.'

Waterbeach Community Primary School

The change in our approach to reading has made it necessary to take the next logical step of looking systematically at our language approach as a whole. We have spent the last year rewriting the language guidelines throughout the school which, now finalized, seem fairly succinct. They did in fact entail considerable and valuable discussion among the staff.

Looking back on the last two years I think that we are confident about the change, without reservation. As teachers we are constantly delighted and excited by the change in children's attitude to reading, their choice of books, their enjoyment and confidence. The once would-be failures are now confident with books and we are able to enjoy reading with them instead of wading through yet another 'parallel reader'. The main frustration for teachers is the lack of time in the school day to give individual children our undivided attention. As always we often use lunch hours and breaks to read with children.

Our daily class reading sessions, lasting about half an hour, are, I think, of considerable value. During this time children are able to become familiar with the variety of books in the classroom; they share books and ideas with each other, often the more fluent readers will read a story to another child, or group of children, or help another child to read. Non-fiction, joke books, rhymes and poems are all very popular for sharing with each other. For the teacher, we can not only share this time with the children but it gives us an opportunity to observe their 'book behaviour' and reaction to different books.

The majority of parents seem involved and happy with the

approach. Some with older children, or those who have come from other schools using schemes, have expressed reservations to begin with, but seem to appreciate the use of real books, often saying how relieved they are not to have to go through those 'boring books' with their child. They become much more involved in sharing a book, often commenting on whether their child or they themselves have enjoyed the book. Concern about the learning to read with real books takes time to dispel, but more often than not the parents are surprised at the confidence with which the child reads, and their attitude towards reading 'difficult books'. Some parents have difficulty finding time to hear their child read regularly, so we try and make arrangements for extra time in school with a parent helper.

The transient army population makes life complicated at times as families arrive in ones and twos. This means that we have to make time to outline our reading approach and for discussion on an individual basis several times a term. However it has its spin-off in getting to know each new parent as they frequently come into the class to discuss how their child is coping.

We still have one or two parents, mainly, I regret to say, university parents, who would prefer to see a more structured approach to reading, in spite of discussions and explanations.

For children leaving school in the infants we felt it necessary not only to send records, which include the comment books and list of books read, but also a sheet explaining our approach to reading, for the next teacher. This is particularly for the army children whose parents expressed concern about the next school.

This problem of continuity between schools often worries teachers. On page 32 are reproduced the notes which Waterbeach passes on with its children's records.

Newlands Spring Primary School in Chelmsford had to contend with a change of staff just when a gradual phasing in of apprenticeship had begun. This has slowed the process but, by supporting each other in a very positive way, the staff have continued to learn and develop an integrated language programme. I was especially interested in Sheila Keenan's comment about catching parents early, at playgroup and nursery stage.

We had a 'vast' changeover in staff in the initial stages and I feel that this did perhaps slow the progress of adopting fully an apprenticeship approach. Those of us who were 'in at the beginning' were certainly keen to establish it throughout the school but as new staff, who were unused to teaching reading in this way, joined the school, we had to sell the approach to them also, which

GUIDELINES FOR READING 1986

We see reading as an integral part of the curriculum with the emphasis on reading for pleasure. The children select a book to enjoy, with guidance where necessary. The book may be `read' at different levels when the child is encouraged to talk, make predictions and reason.

We approach reading through:

1. Talking about the pictures and reading the story to the child.

2. Reading the book with the child while the adult points at the words.

3. Shadow reading in which the child echoes the adult reading.

4. The child runs finger along the print telling the story in their own words, sometimes pointing at familiar and interesting words. Memory plays an important part at this stage.

5. The child begins to point out individual words with the adult filling in words to maintain the flow of the story.

6. The child gradually takes over reading the story using a variety of strategies for difficult words; picture cues, prediction cues, initial letter and phonic cues. Time is allowed for the child to attempt the word. The adult fills in where necessary and these words can be looked at when the story is finished.

It is important that children have experience of a wide variety of books in this approach to reading. The following ways will help the children to become familiar with the books in the classroom.

1. Repitition of stories and books.

2. The teachers reading stories.

3. Parents reading classroom books to children at home.

4. Quiet reading daily, where children look at books, read books and read to each other.

5. Specific books linked with television programmes: e.g., Words and Pictures, Watch and other relevant programmes.

6. Reference books related to topic work including the children's own topic books.

N.B. A child may exhibit different stages of reading behaviour at any one time.

[Waterbeach Primary School: These general guidelines are included in each child's records.]

undoubtedly slowed progress.

From the outset all the children entering the school were introduced to the approach. We always spoke to their parents well before they were due to start school so that the parents were prepared for the shift from a coded scheme and could immediately begin to see the importance of reading with their children.

We feel that now we must extend this by going into playgroups and nurseries which feed the school to explain what we are doing both to the staff and to the parents, since we feel that the term before the child starts school is often too late. Very definite attitudes can already be established like . . . 'you can't read now but just wait until you get to school!' The earlier the parents are with us, the better and easier will be the child's progress in school.

Particular problems have been the uncertainty of staff that the children will indeed 'read'. They have lost the security of Stage 1, 2 etc. and this is further transferred to the parents, who do seem particularly to want to compare their child to little Johnny or Mary down the road. Almost from the start the staff were impressed by the children's enthusiastic attitude to the books and many parents also commented on this, although some were a little suspicious that their children were actually finding the books fun . . . they seemed to think learning could only take place if the books seemed difficult! I personally feel it is important for a school adopting this approach (and indeed any other new ideas) to have the security of knowing that it really works. Listening or reading about the experiences of others can certainly lend that much needed moral support initially, even if you already strongly suspect that the approach must be right.   SHEILA KEENAN

The 'literary immersion' technique practised in schools that have adopted the new ideas most successfully is described with great enthusiasm by a teacher at Rushden Infants, Northants.

We have used the apprenticeship approach for a year now and it has been a most interesting and exciting time.

We began by clearing our rooms of reading scheme books and any books that were unsuitable or in poor condition. I gave the library a list of books I wanted and they have been enthusiastic and helpful. We have about five books per child.

We followed a deliberate campaign of 'stories with everything'. We have wall stories constantly on the go, either made up by the children, or familiar stories illustrated by them. We read stories and poems every day, we also tape stories and poems. We make story games for use with the Language Masters. We are doing problem-solving with stories and have made number games using storybook characters. We have an on-going 'literature table', with a nursery rhyme written out and displayed with related objects, e.g. 'Mary Mary, quite contrary . . . ' with shells, paper dolls, silver bells and a peg doll Mary.

The children borrow books from school and may change them as often as they please.

We began 'Breakthrough to Literacy' at the same time. By the end of the year most of the children were using their sentence makers well, and the sentences they made were interesting and somehow 'literary'.

We have found parents of the reception children generally keen and interested. We involved them from the beginning and many come in to read.

We are pleased with the progress the children have made; a few were reading fluently at the end of the year, all could recognize and join in with some words.

Our favourite books have been the usual ones, *Meg and Mog*, *Dr Seuss*, *Peter Rabbit* (& friends), *Spooky Old Tree*, *Spot*, *Jolly Postman*.

It has been a very happy year for us. In sixteen years of teaching I have never seen children with so much enthusiasm for, and knowledge of, books. They know what they like and why. They are able to choose and to discuss books. Most of them will leave whatever they are doing to read with us. I was reading with a child in our wetbay and the children left their water play and came to join in (dripping water all over me).

We are happily preparing now for our second year of the apprenticeship approach. PAT JENKINS

TAKING STOCK

Once a school has begun the process of change in any part of its curriculum it has a responsibility to monitor and assess the progress that has been made. The timing is a matter of choice, although two schools said they probably wouldn't have done it at all unless I had written and asked for a progress report! The end of the first year seems a popular point for 'first impressions', with a further checkpoint at the end of the infant stage and, for primary schools, at the mid point of the junior years. An adviser I know says, 'The time to take stock is at the end of each generation that goes through the school.' This is perhaps rather too long a gap for a primary school, however!

The teachers whose experiences come next have stopped to take stock at various stages of reading development. They have been remarkably honest in considering the problems as well as the successes; the challenge for them will be to solve these problems as well as to extend the success. In some cases the solutions may be practical, perhaps the introduction of something like Breakthrough to provide the sight vocabulary support they feel is missing; in other cases maybe further experience and growing confidence will provide the help needed.

Here is Margaret Armitage, who is working in a school in Oxford.

I feel it is important to set the context in which the reading has been developing. Last year was mainly concerned with consolidating our earlier work on topic work both in practical terms in the classroom and in more general terms such as in forming guidelines to project work planning. This was our major focus for the year. In addition, we have been reorganizing our reading resources – creating areas for ungraded 'real' books, building up the stock particularly in poetry and picture books. Reading records which were devised in the Autumn term together with a new reading policy have also been under trial. So you can see that a detailed investigation into the apprenticeship approach, i.e., collecting/conducting research evidence has not been possible. However, I have continued with the approach with the class of 7/8 year olds I had last year, 50 per cent of whom have been with me since they began at five and are used to the apprenticeship approach. So, what have I observed?

Advantages
Attitude – this has been the most positive aspect of the change from scheme/colour-coded system. Right through to the 11 year olds, there has been an incredible shift of attitude towards seeing reading as an exciting, pleasurable activity. Even those children who are only at the early stages on the continuum of reading by the age of 8, have not experienced failure, boredom, or frustration. Reading has become something you succeed at, not something you cannot do.

I have also noticed an eagerness to spend time reading, individually or in pairs. Of particular note is the growing ability even at 5/6 to discuss the contents of these books at a deep-structure level. An awareness of authors and illustrators has developed through talking about favourite ones and requests made for other books by the same author/illustrator. All of this has been without prompting. In general, there is a faster rate of development in reading with many children. The earlier stages seem to take longer with certain children, but once the child has achieved some independence, the rate after that is very rapid. There seem to be fewer children with real difficulties than in previous years.

(35)

Skills

Predictions made by the children are more often based on meaning, knowledge of the language system and personal experience rather than immediate fixation upon phonics. Children are more able to make a prediction, i.e., take a risk because the material enables them to do so. You cannot predict that which is nonsense.

Eagerness to talk about the story in the course of reading is increasing, so the books have become the stimulus for thought and language rather than just words to be recited.

We noted a greater interest in books as a source of pleasure by some parents rather than seeing them only as a means to learning skills.

The approach is developing through the school but, of course, it is not a cure-all. There are still children who have not gained the first steps towards independence by 7/8. This is a crucial but problematic stage. Do we call upon the special needs services? What do we ask them to do? Do we attempt to help the child in partnership with a Special Needs Area Support Teacher (S.N.A.S.T.), school and parents but continuing the same approach (which some might say seems to have failed the child) or do we now offer the child more specific help in those areas in which s/he appears to be failing, i.e., whole-word recognition, phonics, etc.? It is at this stage we need the support, the confidence and the commitment to say that the child does not need a lot of what he cannot do and thereby introducing failure into the process. I know from experience that with those children who are delayed in learning to read, the strongest motivating force and the one which confirms for me that the apprenticeship approach is the right one is that these children still *want* to read. No amount of specialist help can supersede that. On the other hand, I also feel it is our professional responsibility to call on all agencies in support of the child when it appears that progress is not as evident as we would hope. Our area is very fortunate in having a S.N.A.S.T. who fully supports our approach and uses it in her work with the children.

We are working towards a full partnership (i.e. parents, child, school and S.N.A.S.T.) in which each supports and develops the work of the other with parent working alongside S.N.A.S.T. and child in the classroom. However, the S.N.A.S.T. is faced with the dilemma of the child at 9 who has gained little independence, very limited sight vocabulary and inappropriate use of phonics. A new tack, something 'special' is needed and she may use schemes such as 'Fuzz Buzz' (I mention this later under 'concerns'). We do not use 'Breakthrough' as a writing/reading support because we do have reservations about it and make greater use of invented spelling, drafting, children correcting spelling errors in the final draft through 'Look-Cover-Write-Check' method etc.

Concerns

The need for the whole school to be committed is vital as well as having good contact with parents. It cannot work in isolation in one class.

Having the confidence to continue the approach even when the child may not be making the expected development is crucial. We need, too, the back-up of research evidence in relation to the children's progress in the later years i.e., after 7. Six children in my class by 8 had not taken first steps towards independence despite parental support, use of 'real' books repeated at the children's request many times, apprenticeship approach and strong motivating factors in the children. Has the barrage of new vocabulary been too great? How could I have developed long-term memory more? These are the questions at the back of my mind even though I know that it is the content of the book, the encouragement to predict/anticipate/think/discuss etc., which is important. Despite talking with these children about words etc. in the context of the reading, they have not absorbed a basic sight vocabulary by 8 and despite the support of the work in writing. I suspect another tack would have resulted in the same outcome, apart from the fact that the children's desire to read would have been missing. I would really love the time to explore in depth of what type and at what time additional help is required by these older children and still using the apprenticeship approach. Putting children onto 'Fuzz Buzz' seems to result in them beginning to recognize whole words but these are not transferred to other types of reading and the vocabulary is so specialized that they rarely meet it in other contexts.

Strategies developed to improve approach

1. Reading aloud to the children much more frequently, 2/3 times a day.

2. 'Come and read to me' is now 'Would you like to share a book with me?' The contact time is much greater (more talking about the content, connections with child's own experience etc.) and of higher quality though less frequent.

3. Ensure that each child has a minimum of 3 sessions a week to read on his/her own or with a friend.

4. We have a dual system of organization of resources – some colour-coded books (best of commercially produced e.g., *Story Chest*) plus 'real books' and increasing the number of shelves with books by children's authors to the stage where these are the major book resource for each class.

5. Less confident children (not necessarily the less able) tend to go to the colour-coded shelves as well as those on the threshhold of independence.

General Remarks
- Children preferring the paired-reading approach tend to select the uncoded books.
- Other children always go to the uncoded shelves and ignore all the rest although they often get a pile of coded books and read through from top to bottom for sheer pleasure.
- Perhaps those taking longer than others to gain independence like the framework and the security it brings and as there are 'real' books to select, their diet is not impoverished.

MARGARET ARMITAGE

Parents are a continuing worry for all teachers, and some feel that the parents are actually misinterpreting what the school wants to do. My experience is that the 'generation through the school' is the most common turning point for such parents. By that time the children have completely changed, any new approach has begun to be taken for granted and the queries become much fewer. It also seems that schools going for the whole-school changeover and making a public attempt to explain themselves are, unfairly, the ones who have had the most criticism. Perhaps the 'we didn't tell them and they didn't notice' approach has something to recommend it after all! There is no doubt that patience and time are needed with some parents and may dictate the speed of change.

Hazel Kenyon, who was a deputy head in Huntingdon, identifies 'anxious parents with high expectations'.

Without a doubt, all of us would like to see the apprenticeship approach continue with our younger children – whilst at the same time remember that children arrive in school at different 'starting points', and teachers need to be aware of this, in order to build on the varied experiences.

One member of staff actually said the apprenticeship approach provides a natural link between nursery and/or home and more formal reading.

One of its benefits is that now *all* children have easy access to books which appeal to *them*. Children who might have struggled in the beginning now have no sense of failure and so begin to experience a great deal of language. Many teachers do refer to the children as having 'a real love of books'.

However, the way forward hasn't been without its problems, and I'm thinking mainly of pressure from parents – some anxious parents with high expectations who *may* set unrealistic goals, reducing their children's spontaneous enjoyment of books – therefore we feel that some parents need to be taught about their children's reading. Not all our parents are able to read themselves and so some children receive little or no parental support.

One parent, found to be collecting 'reading scheme books' off a shelf, said, 'I'll leave the messing about to the teacher, in the school; I'll teach my child to read more successfully this way.' We do have children whose older brothers and sisters have learnt to read successfully with a reading scheme approach and they use this as their argument for *not* following the apprenticeship approach.

Finally, we all believe that children should, within a happy environment, come to find reading a meaningful and pleasurable experience. Sharing a book with one child, or a group of children, for a teacher who has thirty or more infants in the class, makes great demands on her time, as we all know, and so again we strongly emphasize the need for another adult to be working alongside the teachers of our younger children.   HAZEL KENYON

Hazel's experience echoes that of a teacher in Hounslow who quoted one of her parents as saying, 'How do I know if he's reading better than anyone else if I don't know what book he's on?'

Parents, however, are also useful sources of information and support. Comments from home/school record books are one example of this, and they are considered later on (pages 56–62). But two schools sent me examples of questionnaires they used with parents to discover what they thought about the reading approach. This is an interesting way of getting feedback. Parents will make more considered responses on paper than they might at the classroom door, and it is a way of uncovering misunderstandings and problems in communications.

Histon and Impingham School asked parents to answer the following questions.

1. Of what help did you find the information booklet?
2. Have you enjoyed the activity?
3. Has your child enjoyed the activity?
4. What difficulties or problems have you had using the scheme?
5. In what way do you think the activity has been of benefit to your child and yourself?
6. What suggestions do you have to improve the system?
7. In what way do you think the teachers could be more supportive?   SUE DEE

Histon and Impingham School also, unusually, sent me a fascinating document in the form of a questionnaire that Sue Dee had sent out to the staff. She asked them to outline how 'share-a-book' was organized in their classroom and how many families were fully involved. Then they were asked to list problems encountered and to give their honest opinion about the project. This is heady stuff, and the school is obviously one that has a remarkably professional ethos. Such an approach would not work where teachers felt unable to express themselves openly in writing.

Sue then noted for me the suggestions she made to her colleagues in response to their listing of problems they had encountered.

It was from the 'problem' column on the staff questionnaire that I decided I could share some of the ideas I have found helpful in using Share a Book with parents. So I put a few thoughts on paper under the title of

'Do you think that Share a Book needs revitalizing?'

If so here are a few possible suggestions to help give a renewed interest in Share a Book.

Initially, did you stress to the parents that Share a Book must be a commitment if it was to be a successful activity?

Did you give a practical demonstration with the child – discussing, talking before actually reading together? After the first consultation arrange a short second meeting to discuss any problems or queries.

I continued with five suggestions which could possibly help in revitalizing the scheme.

1. Share a Book is a joint effort on the part of the parent and teacher for the good of the child. It may help to encourage more communication between the parent and teacher by including a comments section in the daily Share a Book booklet, e.g., parents' comment: 'We enjoyed this book'. Teacher's comment: 'Great! There are some more books in this series.'

2. If communication through the comments section falls down and a child doesn't return a book for a fortnight without a reason, then probably it is worth asking the parent to discuss any problems with the teacher.

3. When a child changes classes, e.g., becomes a 3rd year, it is an opportunity to discuss with the parents the value of Share a Book and introduce the sheet 'Going On'.

4. To instil an interest within school about Share a Book. The children enjoy relating to their peers their favourite book of the week. This activity could take place frequently or when one thought some new impetus was needed in Share a Book.

5. To remind parents of the importance of the scheme by giving them a questionnaire.

Sue Dee concludes by offering an intriguing glimpse into the future with maths!

As our Share a Book has proved such a success in the past three years in the involvement of parents and their children a colleague and myself started looking at another area of parental involvement. As we were both members of the local Infant PRIME group we had talked of parental involvement in Mathematics but both of us wanted any involvement on our part and the parents', to be of a more informal nature. Was it possible to organize a maths games lending library? The PTA offered us £200 to buy games for a 'Share a Game' system. A parent designed a logo which will be stamped on all equipment. Hopefully by Christmas or early in the spring term the scheme will be in operation. SUE DEE

Finally, we met Beryl Wainwright and Ann Haggard at the beginning of this chapter as they described the way they adapted and set up their reading programmes. Both finished their letters to me with a consideration of the benefits and problems they had found so far. Like Sue Dee, Ann took this summing-up as an opportunity to plan ahead for the future. It seems to me that, even at this early stage, the greatest value teachers have found is in the changed attitude they feel both in themselves, as they understand more about the apprenticeship process, and in the children's response to it. This was certainly my first reaction, too.

Beryl Wainwright starts with:

Benefits
1. The children read for pleasure.
2. The competition for reading levels disappeared and so did much parental pressure.
3. Sharing a book with a child became a pleasure for the adults concerned rather than a chore. Sharing their emotional responses and hearing children read with expression is a delight.
4. Parental involvement and trust improved.
Problems
1. Choosing can become a difficulty for children once they have become fluent readers. They become over ambitious and choose books which need adult support, but they don't feel they want adult support any more. Book covers don't help much. The cover can be misleading and often doesn't tell a child much about the content of the book.
2. Another problem is that many children reach a plateau in their reading and appear to make little progress over quite a while. We have found that they do move on as long as they are given patient support.
3. We give our children a reading test before they leave us to

(41)

move to the junior school. The junior school like a reading age to help them know where to put them back on the Ginn 360 Reading Scheme. Sad, isn't it? Parents don't like it and we hear from parents that our stamina readers begin to get disenchanted with reading.

Anecdotal Evidence

Child reading *Fantastic Mr Fox* insisted we stop reading to turn back to another part of the story. 'Do you know why Mr Fox said that? Because if you look back on page – you will see what happened.' He really knew what was going on.

Another child reading about a cupboard under the stairs, 'We've got a cupboard under our stairs, do you know what we keep in our cupboard?'

Child took home *Peace at Last* by Jill Murphy, shared it with parents. Then his friend came to call. His friend's surname was the same as the elephant in the story, so the two sat and giggled and read several times over.

Parental comment about book taken home for weekend, 'He has walked around all weekend with this book under his arm and read it to anyone who would listen'.

One child felt so confident about his reading ability that he picked up a copy of *War and Peace* at home and tried to read with parents, who were very supportive. Parental comment in record book: 'Tried *War and Peace*, gave up after three pages, we think it will be a long time before he tries this one again.'

BERYL WAINWRIGHT

I know the feeling. One of my seven-year-olds, equally confident of her ability to read anything, is at present reading *Wuthering Heights* with her mother. *War and Peace* yet to come, I presume!

Finally, Ann Haggard's summing-up:

How staff accepted the idea

– I have found that staff coming into the Infant Department, where there is enthusiasm, have accepted and understood the approach readily.

– There has been considerable opposition from JM staff who lack knowledge of how children learn.

– Opposition from top infant staff who preferred the old method and the securities of tick lists etc.

Problems

– The Special Needs Team have tended to insist on a formal approach with reading scheme, flash cards etc.

– Some teachers (including visiting teachers from other schools) have the impression that our method is totally unstructured – that we simply 'read aloud' a lot of stories. It is difficult to explain all that is happening as we work with the books.

– The Special Needs team have encouraged some of our junior staff to believe that the approach works for some but not for all, so we still have problems with staff worrying about their 'slow learners' (quite understandably they are genuinely concerned); they have introduced the 'Fuzz Buzz' scheme to these children!

– Some of our parents still resent the method, especially if their child is not yet fluent.

– Teachers have expressed anxiety about children being unable to tackle unknown text.

How to go forward

1. We propose to hold more fund-raising events to buy books for junior children.

2. There is a possibility that we shall reorganize classes to have all the infants and lower juniors in one site – this should help with continuity.

3. We are to have an INSET day this year – the Language Advisory Teachers will help with the problems mentioned.

4. We now have a 'Language Team' comprising infant/junior staff – all four members are enthusiastic and already show a willingness to discuss the problems.

5. We have an up-to-date infant language policy and an out-of-date junior policy – the Team are to revise this policy as a whole-school language policy – I am sure that there will be a better understanding of the approach resulting from the discussions.

6. I feel that a detailed explanation of our method needs to be written down – such as – 'We read the books before we put them on the shelves' – 'We encourage the children to read with a partner or in a group' etc. – because still visiting teachers say to me – 'But how do you do it?'. I hope that the Language Team will work together to draw up these 'structure-guidelines' and so have a better understanding.

7. We plan to buy videos for parents to borrow.

I have a new job, now, of coordinating the infant department. I am keen to ensure the continuity of parental involvement. This flourishes in the infant department, then wanes when the children move to the new building. ANN HAGGARD

3 Parents

It has already become obvious how often parents appear as problems in teachers' perceptions and how often parents' responses seem to inhibit what schools would like to do. There seem to be two sorts of parent who cause anxiety in teachers (and not just over reading innovation either). The first is the 'pushy parents' who are seen, often, as being middle class, well informed (to excess perhaps) and resistant to any change in education that runs counter to their recollection of their own schooldays. These are the parents who are quoted as saying, 'I learned to read on a reading scheme and what's good enough for me . . . '. The second type is the exact opposite; these are the parents who are described as indifferent to their child's education. They never come to meetings, never read with their child, won't answer letters and are 'just not interested in school at all'. Sometimes they are excused because they are illiterate or speak no English and so 'can't help, even if they want to'.

Both sorts of parent worry teachers who want to change to an apprenticeship reading model; the first because they are so critical, the second because they will not, or cannot, give the children the support that is so desirable in shared reading initiatives.

As Margaret Brooks, an adviser in Doncaster, says, 'Although the apprenticeship model can and does work very successfully, I think that some parents may need help in developing certain skills or understanding, and we can only discover this if the right climate prevails.' Because, as the Bullock report said, 'There is no doubt whatever of the value of parents' involvement in the early stages of reading. What needs careful thought is the nature of that involvement and the attitude they bring to it' and it is obvious that many of the schools quoted in the last chapter have taken great care to involve parents and keep them fully informed. Where they didn't, as at Jan Maxwell's school (page 24), they soon realized the problems this caused. As Jane Richards says, ' . . . it is important to let parents know what is happening, to invite them into the classroom and show them. It is also important to appreciate and give parents credit for all the work they do with their children, to show we value them.' (On the other hand, of course, there is my anonymous headteacher who avoided telling parents anything at all! This is not seen as an option by many schools, however.)

Assuming that we do want to include parents in our plans and to minimize the problems, how have schools tackled the process?

There seem to be two ways of involving and informing parents; in schools where parents are already involved in other ways, through nursery activities or parental help in class, it is perhaps easier than in schools where parents have always been kept at playground's length. I would even suggest that, if your school has never really worked with parents in any way before, it would be better to build up a relationship through parent help with baking, swimming, conventional reading or whatever before trying to introduce a change in reading approach which will rely a good deal on parental support. You need to be seen to be trustworthy, perhaps, before you can be trusted. You will remember that Carrie Sutcliffe came to her Halifax school with a commitment, first of all, to 'develop mother/father/family involvement and develop self identity of the children' *before* she began to work on the reading approach. She is working in a school with 98 per cent ESL families who, it is often assumed, cannot give the school the support that apprenticeship needs. And yet look at the support she has and the way the parents have responded to her imaginative and respectful initiative. As Hertfordshire's excellent booklet for teachers on *Shared Reading* (of which more on page 89) says, 'Parents from all social classes and ethnic groups are able to help their children if teachers are willing to accept them as partners'. (If teachers are unwilling to accept them as partners, then I seriously doubt that apprenticeship reading would succeed at all.) One school that prepared very carefully for the involvement of their parents is Waterbeach Primary. Here is their description of the process:

1. *School Organization*

Our school is a large primary school which is divided into three working units, or Houses, to reduce the scale of relationships for the children and encourage meaningful discussion among the staff. There is a reception class and each house has two vertically grouped infant classes and two or three junior classes. This arrangement may vary from year to year depending on the number of children. Since we have a large intake of army children the numbers fluctuate throughout the year.

The school is a designated community school which means that it is the centre of community life of the village, with adults using the facilities when they are not required for school use.

There is a PTA which runs fund-raising activities and generally supports school events. They also produce a termly journal called

'WHAT', which includes children's work and articles by teachers and parents.

2. Parental Involvement

For many years the philosophy of the school has placed an emphasis on the need to involve parents in the life of the school. The atmosphere is open and relaxed, welcoming parents into school at all times. In most classrooms, parents are involved alongside the teacher working with children in a variety of ways across the curriculum in areas such as cooking, sewing, reading and maths activities. Through this involvement and by being supported and directed by the teacher many parents gain confidence in the classroom situation, and most teachers would probably agree that they offer valuable help.

In a broader context parents have helped with school projects on the outside environment: building play areas and equipment, painting a mural and building a pond. These have been maintained by the parents. Many parents help with class and school plays, for assemblies and large school productions, making costumes, helping with groups of children and making scenery. Events such as Book Week and Summer Fairs often involve parents in school who like to help for a limited time rather than a long-term commitment in the classroom.

Parental Involvement and Reading, July 1987
(Initiating the Change to the Whole Book Approach)
About two years ago we were using colour coding to grade a variety of books, both books from schemes and other books the children enjoyed reading. We realized this was still too restricting, that children would often ask to read books outside the range. Also coding books was a very time consuming process.

We were aware that parental involvement played a significant part in the child's interest and attitude to reading and that we needed to look more closely at the ways we approached reading with children and parents.

These ideas were reinforced at the Parental Involvement Course at Cambridge Institute attended by three infant teachers and one junior teacher.

Following discussion with the staff we decided to change to the whole book approach, with the child making his/her own choice from a wide selection of books in the classroom. (This was assisted by a substantial contribution for books by the PTA.)

We then looked at the following areas which we should consider in developing this approach.

1. To place a value on storytelling and reading.
2. To share books with the children so that learning to read was

relevant and enjoyable. To develop the skills of reading by reading the book at different levels according to the child's needs.

3. To develop the child's writing in topic and story so that it is meaningful for her/him to read.

4. To involve all parents in their child's reading and have a shared reading programme, with parents, children, teachers and other people, with extra support helpers for childen whose parents may not be able to spend time reading with their children.

Thomas Report 1985 P.I. in Children's Reading
It is interesting to note that the Thomas Report included the following comment:

'In the last five years positive action has been taken to engage parents' involvement in the teaching of reading, offering a reasonable amount of training in what parents are expected to do and assuming a voluntary role between school and parent as to their functions. Children take books home to read to parents and return next day with book and any written comments parents wish to make to teachers. N.B. Schools should not enter into this scheme without careful consideration of the effort that will be needed to sustain it.'

Reading – Points to Make When Talking to Parents
1. Compare learning to read with the spoken language; the child learns 2000-3000 words by the age of five years.

Children learn to speak before they can read!

Adults encourage new words, not just repeating one or two words over and over again, but tell the child new words linked with new things and experiences. We speak to children in sentences.

2. Reading is a process of getting meaning.
The teacher's responsibility is to make reading possible.
Children must want to read –
Books must be meaningful – reading schemes narrow down range of meaning with limited vocabulary.

3. Text in books is crucially important and must be meaningful to the child. (Show examples of suitable books, compare reading schemes.)

4. Role of adult – as a guiding friend.
Three parts to play in helping child to read:
  a. Providing a wide range of books for the child to choose from – school, home, school book clubs and shop, library.
  b. The adult's role is similar to helping the child to speak, in helping the child to see what he is reading by reading the story with him.
  – Helping with the words the child does not know.

(47)

– Helping to make reading easy not difficult.

c. The hardest thing to do – withdraw all hint of failure and competition. A child should know what she is going to read.

Allow the child to make mistakes and correct herself from the meaning in the story.

Give the child time. Give lots of praise.

Reading is enjoyable; if the child is becoming tired or bored finish reading the story for him/her.

Children still enjoy having stories read to them at all ages!

5. Introduce comment booklet and talk about writing comments.   WATERBEACH COMMUNITY PRIMARY SCHOOL

Where schools have been working with parents for some time and have a partnership already in place, things plainly become easier. Many of my reports from teachers have emphasized that home/school reading programmes were already set up and relationships established as open and friendly before the change to apprenticeship began, as at Waterbeach. A common response was something along the lines of 'We needed only to explain the change in what we wanted parents to do with books, because children have worked with parents before'.

There seems to be a pattern in the way schools approached parents. The initial contact, assuming an existing basic relationship, was through a meeting with all parents likely to be involved. This may have been informal and individual, as in the case of the teacher who simply caught every parent of the reception class in the playground, one at a time, and spoke personally to them about how to read with their child; or it may have been a more formal meeting, perhaps with a speaker or a video film. Incidentally, I did like one school's approach to the meeting method: the meeting took place at three o'clock. The head took the meeting while the children were still in their classes. In this way parents didn't have to turn out in the evening (often a problem in shift work areas) and were happy to come and listen with a cup of tea (and squash and toys for the toddlers) while they would have been waiting for their children anyway. Two sessions like this caught nearly every family, (especially when it poured with rain on the second day), and the time limit of fifteen minutes concentrated the message to the vital points admirably! Of course the drawback is that in many areas working parents may be excluded; an evening meeting could have been added to involve working mums and dads as well.

The next step is often for some sort of written follow-up to the spoken word. The variety of forms that this can take is amazing, but the message is always the same and consists of reminders of the basic points of apprenticeship. It is, of course, very important that any written notes for parents should be free of jargon and friendly to read. No parent should have to look up 'grapho-phonic' or 'psycholinguistic' after a hard day at work. (I'm not even sure any *teacher* should have to.) Incidentally, an interesting example of what I mean by using friendly language was given to me by Mary Jane Drummond from the Cambridge Institute of Education. When she was a headteacher in Sheffield she set up meetings for parents on reading. Below, you will see the handout she prepared for the first meeting in 1982. Following it you can see the changes that were made by 1984:

Changing Perspectives: how (some) teachers learned (something) about the teaching of reading.
 First Attempt - Summer 1982
Welcome to the reading evening
 We would like to begin this handout for the exhibition by setting down some of the important principles that determine the way we teach reading – and then, on the back of this sheet, there is a section about the way we organize the reading books into a graded scheme.

1. The most important principle is that, from the very beginning, reading should be interesting and enjoyable in its own right.

2. Just as important as the pleasure children get from reading is their understanding of what they have read – from the very beginning. There is no point in recognizing words, and reading 100 per cent accurately, if you don't understand what you have read!

3. We try to emphasize the pleasure and enjoyment to be gained so that children don't see their progress in reading as some kind of a race. We don't want them to waste time worrying about who can read better, or less well, than they do.

4. It's especially important to get this idea over, because all children learn to read at different ages. There really is a tremendous spread across the age range – and it has nothing at all to do with the child's intelligence. Some children start school already reading, some children don't learn to read until they are seven or older.

5. We give the children a lot of encouragement and praise – this helps them to enjoy reading even if they are not making rapid progress. If they once get 'turned off' reading, it is very much harder to teach them.

6. We use a lot of different books, of different kinds, because there are so many different abilities involved in reading. There are many different ways of 'reading' a word, e.g.:
 – recognizing it by sight: the way even very young children read

their own names
- 'sounding' it out, letter by letter, which isn't always reliable!
- using the pictures in the book to guess what it must be
- using the sense of what has gone before to guess what it must be
- using a sense of what will probably come next to guess what it must be
- using a combination of any two or three of these methods.

7. From the last section you will see that we believe there's nothing wrong with guessing! We think it's a powerful way of tackling unfamiliar words, sentences and stories.

Second Attempt – Autumn 1984
Planning the Reading Workshop: our messages to parents
1. We'd like to show you some of the things we do.
2. We want children to read at home with you, as well as at school.
3. Teaching reading is *not* 'best left to the professional'.
4. You know your child better than we do.
5. If you tell us anything that worries you, we'll tell you how we approach the problem.
6. Different children learn to read in different ways, at different ages.
7. There aren't rights and wrongs in the teaching of reading – within limits!
8. We've changed our minds about the teaching of reading – within limits!
9. 'Phonics' isn't the most helpful technique.
10. Reading is about enjoying books, not about reading schemes, reading ages, colour coding, and getting every word right.   MARY JANE DRUMMOND

The difference between the two 'attempts' is instructive. It is not a question of being patronizing but of being accessible, brief and useful. Without this accessibility there may be problems, however willing both parties are to work together. This is a point made by Margaret Brooks, again, when she says:

There is often a difference in understanding between teachers and parents, even though meetings are held and explanations are given about methods, approaches and underlying philosophies. I do feel it to be of great importance that schools create opportunities for parents to meet with staff in small informal group situations where parents can ask for clarification at the level which is appropriate.
    I mention this because of a personal experience I had as headteacher when we founded a parents' reading workshop, planned a series of sessions, which were very well attended, only to

discover that there was a great mismatch between what we were proposing to offer and what the parents needed. This came to light only because of relationships which existed and the opportunity given to parents for free discussion with the chance then of feeding back, anonymously, to the staff and audience.

Aspects such as letter formation, sounding out of letters, sound blends were raised by parents who felt they needed confidence in handling these matters even though we as staff had not considered that parental involvement in helping children to read would encompass these areas, but would be based on the apprenticeship model . . .

I feel also that the schools in the Authority who have begun apprenticeship reading approaches are achieving success, but need contact with and support from other such groups, and I feel any work or project which could be undertaken to disseminate information about successful projects could help not only those schools which have made a start, but also those schools which are contemplating beginning to involve parents in this way.

MARGARET BROOKS

Here is an example of a school which began involving parents by meetings and written follow-up. The interesting thing about this is the way the project spread to other schools even though parental involvement was not part of received educational wisdom in the area.

Perhaps you would be interested in our experiences in South Africa regarding the use of real books in helping children to learn to read.

In the past we found that, while the kids learned to read quite well mechanically, they did not enjoy reading lessons and thus don't read very much on their own. It seems that in most classrooms the cognitive aspects of reading were given preference at the expense of the affective aspects. The Education Department gave us permission to do a project on reading in order to try to get pupils more interested in reading.

We studied your *Read with Me* together with other publications on the teaching of reading and started in January 1986 with our reading project in four schools. In addition to the usual readiness programme, we introduced books from the beginning of grade one (six-year-olds). The paired reading was done by the parents at home as we do not use extra people in the classrooms and the time allocated to reading is limited. The idea was discussed with the parents and the procedure explained during PTA meetings and followed up by letters.

In school we introduced more language-orientated programmes on listening, thinking, talking and discussion. We also put great

(51)

emphasis on incidental reading, that a structured reading programme is essential to ensure that each child gets to the basics of the
decoding skills which are essential for independent reading on a
meta-cognitive level. For this we used the existing basal readers.

M.M. LANCASTER, Pretoria

In every case where parents have successfully joined the
teachers in reading initiatives the schools have worked very hard
to contact and follow up as many parents as possible. They have
also mentioned that there may be a point, with very few parents,
at which you have to accept that, for whatever reason, you are
not going to win. This may be because the parent remains
hostile to what you are trying to do. In which case they can
either trust you or take their child to another school that will
offer what they want; parents cannot, and should not, dictate
teaching methods. (Suppose each of the sixty parents of your
class wanted you to do something different for their child?) It
may be the case that the family is just inadequate. Then it is your
job to try and make up for that, as far as you can, by giving the
child extra support at school. The number of failures that
schools have reported in communicating with parents is
remarkably small, however, and this confirms that goodwill can
find a way through most problems.

It has been impossible to include in this chapter the full texts
of the many booklets for parents that schools have sent me. I
wish I could; many of them are highly entertaining, with jolly
cartoons and drawings by both teachers and children. Instead,
with many thanks to everyone who offered me their booklets, I
reprint, on pages 53-4, several pages from *Reading Together*, an
excellent booklet from Stenson Fields Primary School in Derby.

Finally, let me quote two individual teachers who are working
closely with parents. Both have already contributed to Chapter
Two; the first is Pat Almond, the second Carrie Sutcliffe. Both
teachers are not only working in schools where parents are
asked to help with reading at home, or to read with children in
the school, but they have also developed a more intimate
relationship with parents. They see not only what parents can do
to help the school and the children, but also what the school can
do to help the parent by offering social support, friendship and
security to these mothers and fathers. They make their
classrooms places where parents can come in their own right,
not just for the use the school can make of them. These
imaginative, welcoming partnerships enhance the view the
children have of the value the school places on their home and
family. It must also enhance the view those families have of the
value of the school's activities.

What can parents do to help?

Many parents want to help their child to learn to read, we hope this little booklet will help to guide you in these early reading together stages.

Think of your reading together stages as an "apprenticeship". You, the adult, are a guiding friend, you want this experience to be ENJOYABLE and fun so that the child (apprentice) will come back, time and time again, for more.

REMEMBER — the key word is ....
ENJOYMENT

1. Reading together:
Find a quiet time when you can both relax together.

2. Let the child choose the book. They may like the same one over and over again. This is a stage of learning to read. Often this is the first story your child will learn to read.

MRS WOW WOW
SPOT
A Good Book
BOMMY KNOCK

Pages from the parents' booklet of
Stenson Fields Primary School, Derby
(and overleaf)

3. Sit comfortably and relaxed.
Perhaps side by side on the sofa or sit the child on your knee.

4. Make sure you can both see the words and pictures comfortably. Read the book slowly pointing to the words with the childs finger or your own as you go along. This will get the child familiar with print going from left to right. If the child can join in with you, good, if not — don't worry - they will.

5. When you have finished reading the book let the child "read" the story to you. This may be reciting by heart or making the story up using the pictures, but this is a very important stage of learning to read and can be amusing (for the adult) and fun for the child.

DO

Give lots of praise, we all thrive on encouragement.

Well done!

... Enjoy your reading together time.

At the beginning of the year I found there was not a great deal of interest by many of the parents; some would come and read with their child before the beginning of the session, many were hesitant, some simply wanted to chat to their friends (and in some cases still do) while the children looked at books alone or with each other. Over a few weeks I involved all the children with books, plenty of time was given to story, poetry and singing sessions as well as the children having time to look at books for themselves and to find favourites. I sowed a few seeds with the children by reminding them that whoever brought them to school was welcome to come and read with them before the start of the session and that younger brothers and sisters were welcome too. Slowly more parents became interested (often by their child demanding to be read to). Many have had to overcome fear/embarrassment of reading in front of other adults and children, many seem to be enjoying this sharing time – some sadly do not wish to join in despite their child wanting to be read to and with. One mother in particular who was hesitant found her younger child (all of two years old) eager to read – she watched her brother reading a 'big book' and using the pointer she copied him and was soon reading her own version of stories. She has since graduated on to normal size books and reads with mother for audience and both now enjoy sharing books. This little one will also 'read' to anyone willing to listen if mother is talking to a friend. PAT ALMOND

Carrie in particular is helping parents come to terms with what is for many of them an unfamiliar culture, using her time not only to promote reading but play and social activities.

I have started a parent/school link. Each afternoon parents are invited to the hall to 'play' with their children. The invitation was initially to the reception classes (68 children), but from the start some nursery and middle infants have been involved. Reading has a natural place in its development. On the four afternoons we run, we average 40 parents. Dad's day is Monday, Mum's, Tuesday, Wednesday and Thursday, although some come every day, and this I feel is wonderful. I have seven or eight helpers to play matching games, snakes and ladders, dominoes, what's in a square, and sharing books. At first parents only attended and we had a lovely time, they soon had their favourite games. Last week I introduced the children. We moved story time from home time (another success) so that children could easily leave their classes to join the 'hall scene'. We found that parents were still playing together and children were playing with a helper. Perhaps I introduced children too soon!! This is the situation I really believe I should develop according to the needs of my children and parents with no set ideas but ideals for the future. CARRIE SUTCLIFFE

(55)

4 Keeping Records

A natural follow-up to inviting parents to share in the reading
partnership with their children is to ask them to help with
record-keeping. It is useful, if not vital, to keep track of what
children are reading. This can be a very time-consuming task if
it is not streamlined, especially when you realize that for many
children reading through apprenticeship may entail the reading
of two hundred or more books in a year. Consequently, nearly
all schools who wrote to me have enlisted parents' help in the
keeping of book records. Many have provided the opportunity
for parents, teachers and, more rarely, children to add comments
to the record, so making it a source of communication as well as
information. My only reservation about this is that comments
should not be made obligatory. The burden this can place on
teachers and parents, to find something, *anything* to say, can be
irritating and pointless.

Nearly every apprenticeship school has a booklet of some sort
which goes home with the book the child has chosen in a bag or
folder. The way the book is changed differs a good deal. Some
schools let children change books quite freely as often as they
like; there are many ways of recording who has which book.

Pam McLeish in my own school devised a ticket system. Each
book has a ticket paperclipped inside with the book's title
written on it. On a windowsill is a Breakthrough project folder
with each child's name written above the card holder. As a child
chooses a new book an adult helper takes the ticket out and slots
it by the child's name. As the book is returned the card is
replaced in the book. In this way a check can be kept that every
child has a book and of where every book is. This works so well
that I now use the same system, and my top infants look after
the ticket system themselves.

Other schools keep a firmer eye on book-changing, perhaps
not letting a child choose a new one until the teacher has
checked if the last one was read, or has asked the child to tell
something about the book. I must admit I don't see much
advantage in this. It is time-consuming, slows down the amount
the child reads and has an unattractive air of policing about it. It
is a hangover from the 'we can't trust a child to read a book
properly unless we check up' era but seems unnecessary where a
child is choosing a book he or she really wants to read rather

than one he or she is told to read. Besides which, have we grownups never returned a book to the library half-read?

There is one further refinement that several schools have described to me. They have a system of coloured cards, typically red, orange and green. The red card means 'Please read this to me', the orange, 'Please share the reading with me', and the green, 'Please listen to me read this book'. Bewbush First School use bookmarks:

Every child in our school regularly takes home books to read with his/her parents. The titles of the books are written in the child's 'Bewbush Reading Book' and parents and children are encouraged to comment about their reading in this book. We have found that as the children get older they gradually take over the comments! Younger children also take home a bookmark with a message relevant to the child and the chosen book, such as 'please read this to me', 'I can read this to you' or 'let's read this together'. These bookmarks have been translated into other languages for use by ethnic minority groups in our school.   CAROLYN BANE

Most schools who use this system let the children choose which card they want to take home with their book (thus controlling their own reading input according to how independent they feel that day) but, less attractively, perhaps, one or two teachers made the choice of the card themselves. Again, these seemed to be teachers who found it very difficult to give up the old ways of control over the reading process. For such teachers the card system may well be a useful halfway house before trusting the children to choose what they need. A note was then added to the record booklet of which card was used that day so that an eye could be kept on children who seldom read independently. (It is interesting that very few teachers worried about children who never chose a book to *listen* to . . . although this is also an important part of reading experience.)

The reading record booklet can take several forms. I was interested to see in one sent to me that it was filled in by the child. As children become old enough, there is no reason why they shouldn't take on this responsibility.

Where parents and teachers have commented in these booklets, it makes for fascinating reading. Parents often show a great deal of interest in this recording activity, and it can be very illuminating for the teacher. Here, from Waterbeach Community School, are extracts from several comment booklets.

28.1.87

On Friday Something Funny Happened.

[Teacher's comment] I have encouraged Kelly to talk about the pictures. I think, as the week progresses, she will see more in each picture. You may like to give the children a name and Kelly make up another adventure?

4.2.87

Spot's Birthday Party.

[Teacher] I read the text.

[Mother] The more we read the book with Kelly she recognized a few words, and her little face was a treat to see when we told her how clever she was. She really enjoyed this book.

Today she said, 'I can read now!' Isn't that lovely?

11.2.87

Pooh's Rainy Day.

[Teacher] I read the story today.

[Mother] Kelly is getting a lot more enjoyment out of books than she used to by using the method of 'her picking her own books'. At first I was dubious about this method but I can see now how it *can* work.

[Teacher] Kelly followed me reading and repeated the story after me.

Share a Book – comments if any.

Date week beginning 27.4.88. Please tick and say who read with child at home.

Monday: *Who Sank the Boat?* Mum.

Tuesday: *Spot's First Walk.*

Nicholas enjoyed this book. He remembered the story from last time, also during the holidays the same story was on the television. Comments: Super.

Wednesday: *Not Now Bernard.*

Thursday: *Mr Happy at the Seaside.*

Nicholas enjoyed this book - Mum and dad.

Share a Book – comments if any.

Date week beginning 18.5.88. Please tick and say who read with child at home.

Monday: *Bears On Wheels.*

Very exciting book. Louise read to mummy and James.

Tuesday: *Stickleback, Stickleback.*

Louise read to daddy and James.

Wednesday: *Bruno and the New Bear.*

Louise read half, mummy read the other half. (Comment: 'Lovely story'.)

Thursday: *Blossom.*

(58)

Louise read to mummy – lovely story.
Friday: *The Giant Jam Sandwich.*
Read with daddy, very enjoyable.

From Kemplah Primary School in Cleveland Pat Almond sent me some extracts from her children's notebooks. What I like particularly about Pat's parents' comments is their enjoyment of a book for its own sake. She has plainly managed to interest both children and parents in literature first and learning-to-read second – a rare talent. Paradoxically, teachers who are able to do this find that 'learning' comes more easily the less it is emphasized.

Books Parents Have Particularly Liked to Use with Their Children
Each child had a notebook and the teacher/adult in the classroom wrote down the date and the title of the book the child had chosen with any relevant comments. The parents then responded to their experience with the book by a short note if they felt it necessary. These are a few selected comments.

A general comment to begin!
Mrs W.: A. brings lovely books home.

Silver Buckles.
Mrs S.: Most enjoyable we all got great pleasure out of singing the rhymes.
The Bad-Tempered Ladybird.
Mrs E.: J. has this book at home.
Maisie Middleton.
Mrs E.: J. enjoyed this book, he has this one at home and knows the story very well.
Mrs. M.: Yes, another super book. Greatly enjoyed and she understood it well.
Rosie's Walk.
Mrs W.: Had this book from library, nice easy story.
Mrs M.: Lovely book, good pictures. She greatly enjoyed this, and appreciated the humour.
Mrs B.: This was one of C.'s favourite books at playgroup.
The Snowman.
Mrs W.: A.'s seen film of this book, thought it was lovely.
Mrs M.: M. enjoyed telling the story by the pictures.
George Shrinks.
Mrs M.: Grandad read M. this book. She described it as fantastic. (Well done Grandad!)
When Willy Went to Wedding.
Mrs M.: Lovely book! She insisted that I should read it again and

again. (I did, 5 times.)

Mrs S.: A good story which M. liked. It lasted us for two nights.

Meg and Mog.

Mrs M.: J. seems to really enjoy all the *Meg and Mog* books. I think it's because the books are brightly coloured and a lot seems to be happening on every page. She joins in with me now as I'm reading the *Meg and Mog* books and readily reads the story to me in her own way, only getting a few words wrong.

Mrs S.: We went through this book 3 times. M. likes this sort of story with witches and spells etc.

The Spooky Old Tree.

Mrs S.: We have had this story before months ago but M. remembered it all mostly word perfect.

Gorilla.

Mrs S.: We had *Gorilla* two nights. M. remembered it from several months ago. He will still only listen to stories at home.

Mrs M.: M. liked this book and again joined in with what happened next.

Mrs B.: We all enjoyed this one.

On the Way Home.

Mrs S.: We had this book months ago and M. still remembers nearly everything.

Dogger.

Mrs B.: R. and his sister enjoyed this one. After I had read it R. informed me he had heard it at playschool. He answered questions on the story quite well and remembered all the children's names.

Mrs M.: M. said we might have *Dogger* for two nights instead of one as he liked this story, said he could remember seeing this book at playschool. He even went to bed early so as we made sure we finished. Please find something else with the same effect.

Each Peach Pear Plum.

Mrs S.: This is a really good book one of the best we have had as M. had to really look to find the hidden figures.

A Dark Dark Tale.

Mrs S.: We went through this story twice and at the third attempt M. told me all about the story word perfect by memory.

You Can't Catch Me.

Mrs W.: B. liked this book a lot.

Mrs M.: M. knows this story now off by heart. He will now go through the book giving full story by the pictures and give every detail.

Are You There, Bear?

Mrs W.: B. can nearly say who the animals and toys are on the back page. I find he likes books with animals in.

Mrs B.: Several repeat words this time which R. soon guessed. He enjoyed finding Bear.

Wake up Charlie Dragon.
Mrs M.: We all liked this book, the illustrations are lovely.
Funnybones.
Mrs W.: Funny book but liked it.
Mrs S.: M. really liked this book because *he* asked me to read it twice to him.
How do I put it on?
Mr W.: D. listened to story and pointed to things as I read to her. Shows a lot of interest.
The Christmas Book – Dick Bruna
Mr W.: D. likes this book and said a lot of pictures of baby Jesus and kings are on the wall at school.
Mrs B.: I don't know if we're early or late with this book, he enjoyed the story, just the right length for him. He soon gets bored, but this story was familiar which helps.
Mog's Mumps.
Mr C.: He like the book and he talk about the pictures in it as well.
The Bears who Went to the Seaside.
Mrs S.: Most enjoyable story B. did enjoy it (almost makes you feel better thinking summer is just around the corner!)
Mrs M.: M. enjoyed listening to this story very much. We liked the pictures and she was able to say what happened next.
Mrs M.: We went through the book once in the evening and then M. read it to us at breakfast time. Not only does he remember the storyline but also whole sentences.
Ernest and Celestine.
Mrs S.: We both found it very interesting, lots of details in the pictures to discuss. A very enjoyable read.
Teddy at the Seaside.
Mrs H.: This book is an easy book for E. to read and she enjoys joining in when I read it to them.
What's Left?.
Mrs M.: M. told us the story several times. We all found it very amusing. M. has always liked stories one can join in with.
Mrs M.: J. showed great pleasure in telling me what came next on the pages and pretending she could read the words.
Home Sweet Home.
Mrs M.: I liked this book as much as M.
Dear Zoo.
Mrs M.: M. knew this story by heart. I thought it was lovely. I hope she chooses some more like this.
Lucy and Tom go to School.
Mr W.: While I was reading this D. kept telling me what she does at school.
Mrs S.: We went through this story twice and M. was comparing it with his school.

Mucky Mabel.
Mr W.: D. likes this story when the pig sat up at the table.
Jumping and *Push the Dog* (Red Nose Readers).
Mr W.: D. knows the words in this book when she sees the pictures.
Not Now, Bernard.
Mrs W.: Funny story but enjoyed it.
Mrs M.: M. told me this story with very little prompting. A lovely book for her age.
Mrs M.: Her dad read this to her in such a way that she was in fits of giggles. But it worked – she remembered it.
Mrs S.: The first part of this book is just like our house in the mornings. M. repeated it to me in the morning after reading it to him at bedtime.
Mrs P.: D. loves this book. Because he knows it so well he thinks he can read it.
The Very Hungry Caterpillar.
Mrs W.: Nice little story and also good for counting book.
Mrs H.: For the second time and we have this book at home, she loves all creepy crawlies!
Mrs E.: M. liked this story very much and would like to bring it home again.
Mrs M.: A clever book with holes punched for counting. M. knew everything about the story after reading it once. Told me the thin caterpillar turned into a fat caterpillar and then into a RACOON not cocoon.
Mrs B.: C. has this book at home we bought it for her because she loved it at playgroup.

These extracts from parents' comment booklets are evidence of a genuine dialogue about books. Another sort of record that schools need to keep is the record of the individual child's progress. You may remember that I mentioned in Chapter Two the National Curriculum and the assessment requirements. When following a publisher's scheme or a colour-coded programme it used to be possible to keep a list of the books read, stages reached, or the child's reading level, as a record of the child's progress. The English assessment levels have changed this. As we get further away from the simplistic reading-age definition of children's progress, however, the problem of what we are to record and how we are to record it looms greater.

There is, as yet, no publisher who has produced a spirit master of 'reading behaviour record sheets' or 'key-stage assessment masters', although given time . . . ! At first, the stern puritanical streak in me recognized this as a good thing because it meant that each school had to devise its own ways of recording the markers of progress. This was very important, I thought, because each school's circumstance is different and children progress in different ways.

Certainly, schools have devised a wide variety of record-keeping systems for apprenticeship. The most straightforward is the tick-off list of skills development; the most complex are the pages inviting detailed analysis of behaviour and understanding. However, it does seem that most schools have used the categories of behaviour development outlined in *Read with Me*. This is not because they are too lazy to devise their own, but because in each case the development they have observed follows the same general pattern and, as I have already suggested, this is in the main the development outlined in the National Curriculum. You will see that the same phrases tend to crop up in all the examples below, however they may be laid out. Landmarks such as 'able to listen to a story', 'knows how a book works', 'attempts unknown text with adult help' and so on are common to almost all the records I was sent as well as being direct quotes from the curriculum document. As one head said, 'We tried to find different behaviours or a different order for them but all our children seem to progress through the stages yours did'.

The first example of a progress sheet (page 64), from Water-beach Primary School, is straightforward, needing only a tick to indicate changing behaviour over the child's first three years.

One of the most interesting record sheets was the one devised for Hertfordshire by Rosemary Stubbs and Chris Davis. It is clearly laid out and has room for dates and comments as it is completed. I have included not only the record sheets but also the preamble to them, which I think is a model of clear thinking.

THE STUBBS/DAVIS READING PROFILE

Many teachers have asked us for a simple method of recording reading progress. We offer this profile, which is designed to record teachers' observations of the child's reading development from pre-reading behaviour to fluent reading for enjoyment and meaning. We have included the development of study skills and the growth of recognition of the style and purpose of text. We also felt it was necessary to record some aspect of language development and writing because they are closely linked with reading development.

We hope teachers will use this profile to record and date the gradual progress of the child at each stage, so we have made space for more than one entry in each box. There is room, too, for teachers to make a brief note of any particular strategies they use

READING EXPERIENCE RECORD

	1st week	1st term	1st year	2nd year	3rd year
Enjoys looking at books					
listening to stories					
Has a wide experience of books at home					
school					
Behaves like a reader					
Pretends to read					
Follows text with adult support					
Shadow Reading					
Chooses books carefully					
Attempts to read known text					
Chats about story					
Shows understanding					
Beginning to predict					
Finger pointing					
Reads known words					
Attempts unknown words					
Can read familiar text with little help					
Uses contextual clues					
Uses phonic clues					
Recognizes and can pick out sight words in known text					
Enjoys rhyming books					
Beginning to read independently					
Can predict events					
Reading shows self-correction					
Able to scan ahead					
Can sustain private reading sessions					
Confident with books					
Not confident with books					
Has favourite book					
Can discuss stories with comprehension					
Is 'book' orientated					
Reads fluently aloud					
Enjoys fiction/non-fiction					
Enjoys reading poetry					
Can use reference books					
Has extra help with reading					
Has specific reading problems					

Waterbeach Reading Experience Record

for the child who needs extra help. On the back of each sheet we have listed books which we think children should be able to read as they progress through each stage. We took these books from Cliff Moon's *Individualized Reading* booklist. We suggest that teachers may prefer to make their own list from the books they use in their classrooms. We have included some reading scheme books and several storybooks so that the child has plenty of choice. We also felt that it is important to record the child's own favourite books at each stage.

The concepts we have used are based on the system used by Liz Waterland and on our own observations. There are two concepts which require further explanation. The third box in Stage 2 records the link between growing confidence in reading and play. We have noticed that children who are beginning to enjoy reading like to act out their new experiences. They pretend to read to their dolls, organize 'libraries' and 'schools' with their friends, and fold pieces of paper to make 'books'. This is not book-making directed by the teacher, but a play activity initiated by the child. The 'books' will have drawings and random letters and words written in them, and the child may ask an adult for help with the writing of a name or phrase.

In the sixth box in Stage 2 we highlight a strategy used by adults and children alike when confronted by a difficult piece of text. We sometimes repeat aloud a sentence or phrase using different emphasis and inflection several times if we are unsure of the meaning of the words. This attention to the rhythm of the prose is a strategy we have noticed children using, sometimes when they are reading aloud to an adult, or when they are reading silently, just beginning to internalize their reading.

We have not attempted to tie the four stages to chronological age, although we expect the normal child to have reached Stage 4 on transition from junior to secondary school. We decided not to number each box, because children develop reading skills in many ways. We felt that the teacher's own dated observations were a better indication of progress than an artificially imposed hierarchy.

The Stubbs-Davis Reading Profile is now published by the Open University in *Shared Reading in Practice* by Rosemary Davis and Chris Stubbs, O.U., 1988. One sheet from this is reproduced, with permission, on page 66.

Another school which sent me very detailed records was Chetwood Primary in Essex. Angela Richardson wrote to me:

Our reading record [page 67] stems from your own 'wheel' and also the Stubbs/Davis language profile. We started using the wheel in isolation but found interpretations differed, therefore space for

Stubbs/Davis Reading Profile	Stage 1	
Name of child:	Age at start of record:	School:
Is able to listen to story. Is aware of plot and pictures. Has favourites. Enjoys choosing books with adult help. Likes visiting library or bookshop.	Is eager to share books. Knows how a book works, e.g. gets it right way up, turns pages, opens book at beginning.	Behaves like a reader. Browses, looks at pictures, talks about books, is beginning to discriminate. Can read story through pictures.
Shows interest in text. Knows that story is told in text. Points to own name. Recognise individual words.	Moves finger underneath words or follows with eyes while adult reads, or when browsing. Recites story from memory.	Begins to repeat words of well-known book, looking at text. Joins in with adult reader. Fills in missing word.

© R. Stubbs, C. Davis, 1987.

ATTITUDES THROUGH SCHOOL CAREER	YEAR			YEAR			YEAR			YEAR			COMMENT
	T1	T2	T3	T1	T2	T3	T1	T2	T3	T1	T2	T3	
Able to listen to story													
Has favourite books													
Has favourite authors													
Prefers fiction													
Prefers non-fiction													
Enjoys choosing books (A) or (I)													
Buys from school book club or													
Shown interest but unable to buy books													
Appreciates books as presents													
Enjoys visiting library (A) or (I) - School													
" " " - Local													
Uses library independently													
Eager to share books													
Browses													
Can read story through pictures													
Prediction													
(Confident in talking about books) sharing with others													
Uses previous experience to analyse new words													
Is able to read aloud with expression													
Is self-correcting Y/N, NN - No Need													
Enjoys variety of style, plot, character													
Tells stories using story-telling lang.													
Re-tells favourite stories selecting key elements of character and plot													
Can review books with a clear idea of preference (and reason)													
Knows work of individual authors													
Private reading - sustains Y/N													
Private reading - enjoys Y/N													
Skim & scan													
Critical Skills													

Chelwood Primary School Reading Record

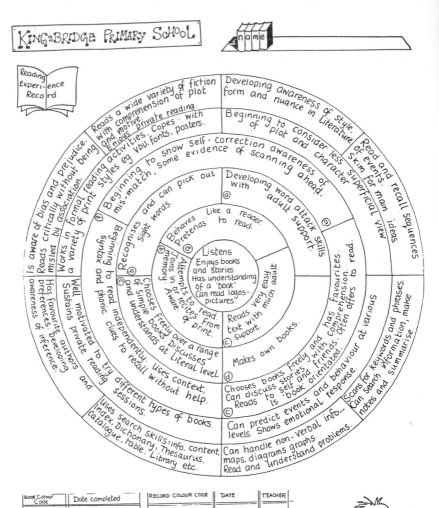

KINGSBRIDGE PRIMARY SCHOOL

name

Reading Experience Record

The wheel chart contains the following text (from centre outwards):

Centre: Listens. Enjoys books and stories. Has understanding of a 'book'. Can read logos-pictures.

Ring (inner):
- (a) Behaves like a reader. Pretends to read.
- (b) Attempts to read. Joins in or recites from memory. Aware of print.
- (c) Reads very easy text with much adult support.
- (d) Makes own books.

Next ring:
- (a) Recognises and can pick out sight words.
- (b) Beginning to read syntax and phonic clues to retell without help.
- (c) Chooses freely over a range of simple books. Discusses and understands at Literal level. Uses context.
- (d) Chooses books freely and has favourites. Can discuss stories with comprehension. Reads to self and friends. Is 'book' orientated. Often offers to read.

Next ring:
- (a) Developing word attack skills with adult support.
- (b) Beginning to show self-correction of mis-match. Some evidence of scanning ahead.
- (c) Well motivated to try different types of books. Sustains private reading sessions.
- (d) Can predict events and behaviour at various levels. Shows emotional response. Can handle non-verbal info- maps, diagrams graphs. Read and understand problems.

Outer ring:
- Reads a wide variety of fiction with comprehension of plot and motive. Enjoys private reading. Copes with private reading activities eg. VDU, fonts, posters.
- Developing awareness of style, form and nuance in Literature. Beginning to consider less superficial view of plot and character. Read and recall sequences of events. Skim for main ideas.
- Is aware of bias and prejudice. Reads critically without being misled by association. Works in formal reading a variety of print styles.
- Has favourite authors. Developing preferences. Developing awareness of inference.
- Uses search skills: info, content, Index, Dictionary, Thesaurus, Catalogue, Table, Library etc.
- Scans for keywords and phrases. Can search information, make notes and summarise.

Book Colour Code	Date completed
Red	
Yellow	
White	
Dark blue	
Pink	
Brown	
Green	
Grey	
Orange	
Black	
Beige	
Dark Pink	
Pale Blue	

RECORD COLOUR CODE	DATE	TEACHER
RED— LOWER INFANT		
BLUE – UPPER INFANT		
GREEN – LOWER JUNIOR		
ORANGE – UPPER JUNIOR		
JUNIOR STANDARDISED TESTS		

comments was needed . . . For the youngest children we also use a sheet entitled 'Reading Development' which is a more detailed record of the earliest stages, and has proved useful for parents.

ANGELA RICHARDSON

I was also interested to see the record of the child's attitudes to reading and careful record of the development of library and study skills.

The 'wheel' form of record has been taken up by several schools and adapted, as it should be, to the needs of their staff and children. Sue Ruffell at Kingsbridge Primary School in Devon sent me her adaptation of the record wheel. She is intending to go even further with it, though, and to produce maths and topic records in the same format. Here, out of interest, is their general language development record and the topic record.

Finally, on pages 70-1, is an example of a pictorial record sheet used by the nursery at Braeburn Infant School, Scarborough. The interesting point about these records is that the staff share them openly with the parents. That is, they are not only shown to the parents but they are invited to help to fill them in. Highlighter pens are used to colour the flower as the child progresses, and sections can be dated. These records provide a focus, enabling parents to become actively involved in observing and recording their child's achievements. I like particularly the deliberate link between developmental reading and developmental writing. This is a link more and more schools are making.

Caroline Matusiak, the nursery teacher (and now at Filey C.E. Infants School in Yorkshire), gave me the rationale behind her record-keeping:

LITERACY FLOWERS

The flowers share the same root to show that the development of reading and writing in the nursery is not only simultaneous but also interdependent. In the holistic approach, literacy can be incorporated within all areas: paper for maps in the construction toys and pencils attached to easels to record ownership of paintings. **The reading flower** records concepts about books, reading behaviour using picture cues and familiarity with book language. The idea of print as communication partly depends on the development of social skills and is indicated on the flower by 'looks at books with friends'. The enjoyment of books at home and at school is central.

The writing flower also records concepts about print. Asking questions about environmental print is a feature of early writers

(69)

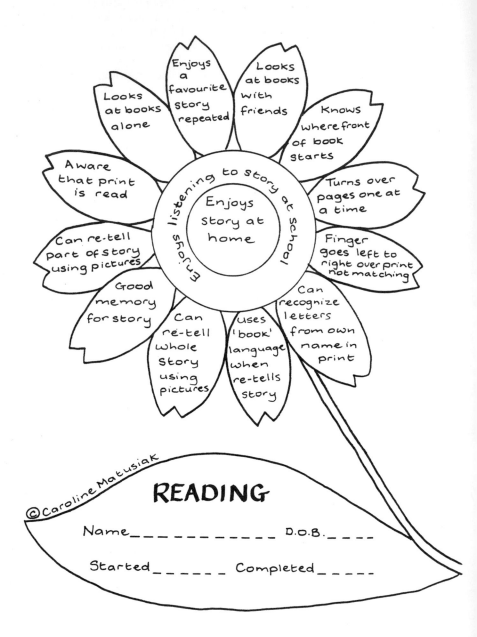

Looks at books alone

Enjoys a favourite story repeated

Looks at books with friends

Knows where front of book starts

Aware that print is read

Enjoys listening to story at school

Enjoys story at home

Turns over pages one at a time

Can re-tell part of story using pictures

Finger goes left to right over print not matching

Good memory for story

Can re-tell whole story using pictures

Uses 'book' language when re-tells story

Can recognize letters from own name in print

© Caroline Matusiak

READING

Name_____ D.O.B._____

Started_____ Completed_____

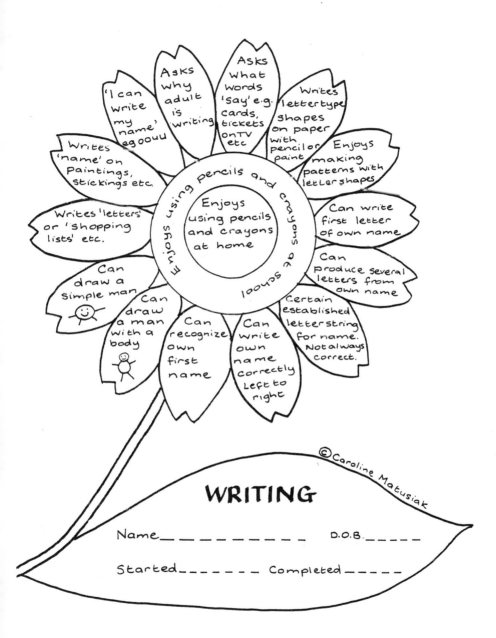

Asks why adult is writing

'I can write my name' egoouu

Asks what words 'say' e.g. cards, tickets on TV etc

Writes letter type shapes on paper with pencil or paint

Writes 'name' on Paintings, stickings etc.

Enjoys making patterns with letter shapes

Writes 'letters' or 'shopping lists' etc.

Enjoys using pencils and crayons at home

Can write first letter of own name

Enjoys using pencils and crayons at school

Can draw a simple man

Can produce several letters from own name

Can draw a man with a body

Can recognize own first name

Can write own name correctly Left to right

Certain established letter string for name. Not always correct.

©Caroline Matusiak

WRITING

Name_____   D.O.B._____

Started_____ Completed_____

and readers. Children demonstrate their understanding of the functions of print to aid memory and transfer information by writing shopping lists and letters. The ability to write letter-shapes indicates not only a growing awareness of the forms of print but also the refining of hand-eye co-ordination. Drawing a man with a body generally indicates that children can represent and are ready to accommodate other symbolic systems – in particular, reading.

One of the first words that a child reads is her name. The ability to produce several letters from it indicates increasing visual discrimination. It becomes apparent that directionality is established not only when the finger goes from left to right but also when children write their name correctly. Children start to notice and comment on letters written in the wrong order, showing a growing awareness of the fixed form and public nature of print.

The flowers provide a focus for parental involvement. They inform parents about the attitudes, skills and concepts that underly early literacy. Children's concept of themselves as writers and readers benefits from their parents' active interest and encouragement. Parents are equally able to appreciate and work with school policy, providing complementary mark-making and story experience at home.   CAROLINE MATUSIAK

This seems to me to combine partnership with parents, help-fulness, ease of use and entertainment to an admirable degree.

5 Special Needs

In a document entitled *Curriculum and Practice in Reception and Infant Classes* produced by Cambridgeshire L.E.A. occurs the interesting phrase, 'all children are special; some have more needs than others' This chapter is concerned with the some who have more needs than others. Does this mean that they have quite different, special, needs which other children do not have? Or does it mean that their needs are the same as others', only greater?

The answers to these questions affect profoundly the way in which we deal with children who do not progress with the same ease as others. If we believe that they have quite different needs from the majority, then, if the majority can learn to read with apprenticeship, presumably we must provide a different system for these exceptions. If we believe that 'special needs' children have the same needs as everyone else but just require more help for much longer, then, again presumably, they too can learn to read through apprenticeship like everyone else.

I have the very strong impression that most teachers and special-needs experts would claim that some children have needs different from the majority. The usual view is that apprentice-ship is fine for the normal child but that children with problems must have 'structure'. And by that teachers don't mean the structure I describe as being integral to apprenticeship development; they mean the structure provided by a published programme of phonics and graded books.

Now if you have read the second edition of *Read with Me* you will know that this is not my answer to the special-needs question; I believe that children who are slower to come to independent reading, whether through intellectual, emotional or physical handicaps, do not have different needs from other children. They seem to me just to need far more of what other children get, and for longer. So many of the children I used to worry about have 'come right' since I have had the experience and the courage to allow them an extra year or so, or to give them extra book input, rather than revert to conventional skills-based teaching, that I am feeling more convinced about this every year.

However, and it is a big however, I am not an experienced special education teacher and, compared with the problems some children have to face, my children find life relatively straight-forward. For that reason I think I initially accepted, for lack of evidence to the contrary, the received wisdom about a need for external structure for problems such as dyslexia, hearing impairment or Down's syndrome, to give three examples.

Then I began to come across evidence to the contrary. The first suggestion that there was more to this than met the eye came in *Cushla and her Books* by Dorothy Butler (Penguin). This remarkable book describes how a handicapped child learned to love books and to read them by being read to in a typically apprenticeship approach. Then I began to hear from teachers who had decided to offer children with learning problems an apprenticeship and supported environment, and had discovered not only that this fresh start was psychologically liberating for the child and the teacher but that it also produced the learning they had previously failed to achieve.

Finally, to convince me absolutely that children with problems need to be enabled to be readers before they are taught to read, just as all children do, I heard from Felicity Craig, the special education teacher at Dartmouth Community College. She works with dyslexic children who have totally failed to make sense of the formal teaching they have had and who are, in their own eyes and those of the schools, complete failures. For years she has been offering them a restart as supported readers, reading both children's literature and their own dictated or typed texts. When they have made sense of the print process and its meaning for them personally, Felicity then works at the specific input they need to spell, write and read aloud for themselves, as we do with all our children. Felicity has written several excellent booklets about her approach to special education which may be ordered from her at 33 Newcomen Road, Dartmouth, South Devon TQ6 9BN.

In one of Felicity's letters to me there is a passage with something very important to say to all teachers. It has implications for all language teaching and has influenced me strongly in what I ask my children to do when they read. The discovery that silent reading and reading aloud are *quite different things* is liberating to strugglers. They can often read perfectly well to themselves. The necessity to *perform* is what produces the problem.

At Dartmouth Community College we try to make the entire curriculum as accessible as possible to as many children as possible within their neighbourhood school.

We try to tackle any literacy problems first and foremost, feeling that this in itself will go a long way towards making the curriculum accessible. The idea is that there are four different kinds of words in everyday use, made of four different 'materials'. Seen words are patterns of visual shapes. Heard words are patterns of sounds; uttered words are patterns of vocal sensations, and we also have physical patterns of handwriting movements.

Any one of these words can convey meaning directly, without any necessary reference to any other kind of word. Totally deaf people, for instance, can read and comprehend perfectly, without reference to 'inner speech'. So we maintain that real reading is understanding print, it's silent, and it is an entirely separate process from the ability to read aloud.

This means that if a child is being read *to*, and he is following the print at the same time, he is having the experience of real reading right then and there, just as fully as if he were reading independently. (I.e., he is associating written words directly with meanings.) So our first task is to provide massive reading input for all reluctant readers, in any way we can. We encourage parents to read to their children, for sheer enjoyment; we provide a large selection of real books, with matching word-for-word tapes; we enlist the services of volunteers, and other children. Whatever! And, we never give up. The beauty of this approach is that the child's 'performance' doesn't matter. His *experience* of reading does – he can't have too much of it. The approach is also very positive: reading 'failure' ceases to exist.

'Saying written words aloud', on the other hand, involves a matching process between patterns of shapes and patterns of sounds. The ability to do this can – and often does – happen at the same time as understanding print, but it may not, and it doesn't have to. Exactly similar matching processes are involved in learning to speak (matching heard sounds with uttered sounds) and learning to spell (matching seen words with handwriting movement words).

Felicity has outlined her approach to spelling and writing problems in far more detail in her booklet *The Natural Way to Learn* (1 85421 063 7). She goes on to say:

Once we assume that the blockage is a literacy problem (i.e. 'dyslexia'), *not* a difficulty in learning as such, it becomes easier for us to see how to include the strugglers in mixed ability mainstream lessons. Pair a struggler with a middle ability student, and let the struggler copy out his 'tutor's' notes, with some reading help if necessary. Good practice in reading and writing for the struggler, plus a positive experience of the lesson; and not much extra work for the tutor. Both students emerge with a sense of achievement; both are learning that education is a cooperative undertaking, not a rat race. The tutor should receive ample recognition and encouragement from the class teacher for the 'tutee's' progress.

But the heart of my job is my work with parents. I now work with individual families (ideally, mum plus dad plus child) on one or two evenings a week, as I've discovered that most parents of secondary age pupils find it difficult to come in during the day. I spend about forty-five minutes with each family, working from 7.30 p.m. until 9.00 p.m.

We always try to get the reading established first, aiming for about twenty minutes reading every day, five evenings a week. Then I show a parent how to help with spelling work, and recommend ten minutes a day on that. This is only a rough guide, and of course is flexible. We arrange appointments every six weeks or so, until the parents are confident. I find it easy to involve parents because I always begin by assuming that parents know a great deal more than I do about teaching their own child. 'Look what you have done!' I imply admiringly. 'Look how much you have already taught your child. Teaching him literacy, in comparison, is as easy as falling off a log. You are probably doing a great deal of it already. Just carry on. Don't test him – don't 'teach' him – simply arrange massive literacy experience for him. Read to him if you are both willing. If not, rush out and invest in books and matching tapes. Then, we'll build on that.' And we do.

Some parents/volunteers become very interested in the whole programme, and offer, for instance, to 'adopt a child in science' – coming in to all his science lessons, helping with any reading and writing, and one homework a fortnight. The volunteers often enjoy the science lessons themselves!

To sum up – the apprenticeship approach to reading is, to me, the breakthrough. You can establish *all* children as real readers – immediately! Dyslexia Associations, fully aware of the crucial importance of a phonic approach to spelling, often assume that phonics is the best route to reading as well, but of course reading takes a painfully long time to establish when approached via phonics. If we can combine the apprenticeship approach to reading with the strong phonic approach to spelling advocated by Dyslexia Associations, and involve parents whenever possible, I see no reason why we shouldn't be able to meet all literacy needs within a normal school timetable.   FELICITY CRAIG

Since my first contact with Felicity I have heard from several other teachers of children with problems who have found the same way to prevent, or rescue the children from, the feeling of complete failure that conventional approaches leave them with. They are still in the minority in teaching but the evidence to support them is increasing, although there are still teachers who find themselves, having problems with specialist staff.

Although I feel that this approach is particularly suited to those children who in the past have been considered failed readers, that is those of junior age and above who do not appear to be succeeding, it is in this area that I feel we have faced more noticeable difficulties, in that support staff such as Special Needs teachers from outside the school or educational psychologists are still a little suspicious of the approach and seem to believe that these children must have a highly structured approach (i.e., a scheme and a good dose of phonics). The class teachers, already nervous of a new approach, are often made to feel that they do not have the same knowledge as these 'specialists' and tend too easily to be convinced that the support staff know best, when in fact they have a limited or non-existent knowledge of this approach. Therefore we never really find out how well the approach works for these children, since the teacher may well abandon it at the first sign of criticism.

SHEILA KEENAN

Another worry is with the local psychological and learning support services. Some of these professionals seem to hold the view that reading with real books is not the way forward for children with learning difficulties. We have also found that on leaving our school children may be put onto reading scheme books.

However, as a staff we are convinced of the benefits of this approach to reading. We appreciate the children's interest in books, their enjoyment of quiet reading sessions, the lack of competition in reading and the sheer pleasure for us all of reading real books.

CAROLYN BANE

It is also true, however, that many special-education staff have told me of *their* frustration when they have wanted to take an apprenticeship approach into a formal school. Plainly the problems are very great when a teacher only drops in on a class for short periods and has different ideas from the class teacher about what the children need. I am inclined to wonder what real good such visitations do when there is a conflict of philosophy. Where the match between school and support teacher is right, or where compromise can be reached, the children have the best chance of benefiting from the support teacher's work.

Here, then, are the voices of some teachers who are concerned with literacy problems and who are also apprenticeship teachers.

The first is Christine North, who was brave enough, when a student, to work with children who were struggling in her teaching practice school.

(77)

My last teaching practice involved using the 'apprenticeship reading approach' with reading scheme books. I found the children relaxed more when they found I did not make them repeat words. When I read for them, children soon learnt to step in where they were able, and to stop for me to read when they were unsure. The class teacher found that when a child starts using this approach, instead of the old way of correcting and sounding out, their reading improves. Reading scheme books are not ideal for a reading partnership. To be a partner in reading, however, I found does reduce the feeling children have of not being able to read, which I found was common in those struggling through a reading scheme.

I took a lot of books into school and tried putting some in the centre of the children's tables. This resulted in the reading of a variety of books which would not have been chosen by the children themselves. It also encouraged a number of children to read who never looked at a book unless directed to do so. The level of the readers' and listeners' heads I have found to be important with the age group 7/8 years. When they were at a lower level than myself I noticed they were keen to finish, yet, when I made them sit on a higher chair while I sat on a lower one, a child tended to stay content longer. I found the length of time a child wanted to read also depended on what they were reading, i.e., no interest in reading scheme books compared to a desire to read more with books I had taken in, or with central library books. A popular practice was to leave reading scheme books at home so that another book could be chosen for reading.

I started teaching in September 1987 in a first school in Bradford. The children are five and a half years old. The school uses *Story Chest* and Link-Up, Ginn plus storybooks. I introduce a variety of good books with the children I teach via library resources, the teaching centre, and through the variety of books to be found in school. Reading is an important part of the day. Children learn through a dual approach: picture books; listening to older children reading; listening to other adults and myself reading; also through words and sentences in their environment.

Children begin writing/reading from their own experiences, and I find those who experience their own words and write for themselves are keen writers and readers. . . . Good books create their own interest.   CHRISTINE NORTH

Many of the teachers who wrote to me are advisory or support teachers like Mary Cooper from Wiltshire.

Because we work with so many different schools, we find it difficult to be other than eclectic and flexible in what we recommend. However, since we all read *Read with Me*, there is a detectable change in our attitude and in our book-buying policy. We still find it necessary to have copies of reading schemes in our Resource Centre because team members need to be knowledgeable about what is good (and bad) in the materials that publishers are promoting. On the other hand, we were the first Support Team in Wiltshire to join our county's library scheme and so have expanded our stock of good quality picture books both by library borrowing and by book purchase.

One of our prime concerns now with struggling readers is to ensure that what we offer them to read is worth their efforts. We have good informal exchange of information about books which have gone down well and also try to keep a written comment in the Resource Centre in a notebook which lives on the bookshelf with the books. Team members now have stopped wanting the books to be colour-coded, as they feel they know more about their interest and reading levels than a readability age would tell them. We are also increasingly involved with setting up situations which offer supported reading to less gifted readers – i.e., paired reading with parents at home, with other children, with volunteers in school, etc., etc.

I wouldn't say that we'd got the reading problem cracked yet. What worries us most is those schools which don't seem to do *any* kind of planned teaching of reading but expect that simple contact with books (reading schemes, 'real' books or whatever) will make all children readers. It may work for some, but Special Needs children in particular need more carefully planned teaching. That's what we're now working on.   MARY COOPER

You will notice that Mary certainly does accept that carefully planned teaching is needed, and of course needed by all children (there *is* a structure), but that those plans should not be rigid and scheme-based. A member of the same team, Barbara Black, told me about David.

David is an eight-year-old who is severely disturbed. He will be transferring to a residential school for the maladjusted in September. His concentration was non-existent and his attitude to reading very, very negative.

I adopted the apprenticeship approach in the hope that this method might introduce him to the pleasure and fun books can provide. He chose books freely and chose *repeatedly* such books as *Where is the Green Parrot?*, *Funnybones*, *Where is Zip?*, *The Hungry Caterpillar*, Dr Seuss books etc. This freedom and repetition provided him, for the first time, with the satisfying experience of succeeding. For much of the time initially, he would not even look

(79)

at the print, but gradually he became more interested. His attention improved, and we were able to make his own book based on *Where is the Green Parrot?*, entitled *Where is David?*! He gained pleasure and meaning from his own language.

A very meaningful start . . .   BARBARA BLACK

Another account of one particular child came from Mary S., who had been working, as a private teacher, with James.

I am a retired teacher with experience in English as a Second Language and remedial work and now have four private pupils. One, James aged twelve years when we first met, had his early schooling in the Far East. On arrival back in the United Kingdom he had some remedial help in a junior-school special unit for one and a half years and then was in remedial bands and had remedial help at secondary school. I was involved as private teacher (for one hour a week) from the beginning of his second year at high school (he has just finished his fifth year).

His reading ability was very poor, very simple words only and his manner (not unnaturally) was rather surly and unco-operative. The first few weeks of that Christmas term were devoted to work on phonics which proved very difficult for him (I used Stott and Gibson). He, I began to realize, had, with so little reading ability, no understanding of the phonic sounds and although the simpler words were readable he had no idea of how to spell that same word.

As I was trying to find a way through this knotty problem I read *Read with Me* from cover to cover on a long train journey. Not only was it very interesting, it immediately struck a chord with my early days as a parent (before becoming a teacher) and the way in which, from ignorance, common sense and/or innocence, I'd helped my own children to read before starting school. On my return I discussed the book and ideas with James's mum who is a teacher and who was interested. She was, I think, by this stage desperate about his reading but was also very supportive of him – so we gave it a try.

Results were fairly rapid in appearing, if only because it cleared some of his hurdles. Since the 'that's too hard for you' syndrome didn't apply, he chose a book that interested him and, of course, we read it together as outlined in Liz's book. This continued with further books and as he became more familiar with words and reading his phonic awareness and understanding also steadily improved (as did his motivation here and at school) and he was able (as he had not been before) to break down and build up new or difficult words. This also resulted in a greatly improved ability to spell. He's now able to take an 'educated guess' at a word he can't remember and he can 'think his way through' the spelling – something he'd no notion of how to set about before.

He's fortunate in that he's got a good oral vocabulary which helps him and has a lot of support from his parents. Another advantage of this way of working with remedial teenagers, incidentally, is that it can be very difficult to find good interesting stories which they are able to read and wish to read. 'Simplified' stories, unfortunately, appear to children with a 'reasonable' intelligence but a very poor reading ability as very condescending and rather a turn-off.

While James hasn't yet reached his chronological age he's narrowing the gap all the time. Some weeks ago after he'd tackled some hard reading very well, I said, 'You've no idea, James, how much pleasure it gives me to hear you read like that!' He replied immediately, 'You've no idea how much pleasure it gives me to be able to read like that!' I can only say he isn't given to such comments!

He hasn't yet turned into a bookworm, although he is much more motivated towards reading than he was (understandably, I think) and is much more able to cope with what is required of him at school.

For the last twelve months he has been compiling a folder for GCSE. Taking this exam has proved to be quite an incentive as there was a distinct possibility that he would have to content himself with City and Guilds. He has written something like half a dozen pieces of 500–1000 words and has managed quite well. The preliminary discussions have been vital and over this period his confidence in his ability to put words down on paper has markedly improved. Given sufficient facts or experience he can develop some good descriptive writing. His main difficulty at the moment is in setting down personal opinions and arguments.   MARY S.

Two more examples from support teachers show how they are trying to give these 'failed' children the new start they need. The first, Linda Prior, was a support teacher in London at the time she wrote.

With regard to my own philosophy, I have been using many elements of the apprenticeship approach for a number of years. The centre I work at caters for children who have reading and related difficulties, including dyslexic pupils, often combined with severe emotional problems from the age of seven, the majority being boys. Over one hundred pupils attend the centre, either for one, two or three half-day sessions per week for an average of two years.

Clearly, many complementary strategies are used to enable

children to overcome their reading difficulties, but of overriding importance is the need to make reading a pleasurable experience for each individual child.

To this end I have always given my pupils free choice on their reading material. Although many reading 'schemes' are available, I never insist on a linear progression throughout any of the elements. Indeed, many children choose 'real' books, either fiction or non-fiction, combined with individual reading scheme books which appeal to them at the time.

I feel that it is absolutely essential that a child feels secure and physically comfortable whilst reading. Very often this means we squeeze up together in a rather tatty but comfortable armchair or sit or lie on the carpet. The younger children often prefer to sit on my lap and, in my experience, older children enjoy the physical security of an arm around them whilst reading, although some occasionally reject such contact.

Reading only constitutes one part of our work and many different activities are used to establish meaningful relationships with the children, for example many types of play activities: cooking, art and craft, shared writing, use of the computer, particularly as a word processor and so on.   LINDA PRIOR

Here is Ann Nosowska talking about a term she spent working with parents on a literacy project.

Since much of my time was spent working with children with reading difficulties I also used the apprenticeship approach with them.

I am convinced that many problem readers have difficulty because they have never gained the concept of reading before being bombarded with skills, and the only logical first step in any remediation is to use the apprenticeship approach. So I always do so and I find that the children's attitude to reading changes as soon as they discover that they can actually make some sort of response to a book. It is also a good way of relieving parental anxiety about reading because as soon as they are involved as 'supporters', rather than 'examiners', in the process they realize that their child *can* make sense of reading after all.

In some schools I had volunteer helpers who followed the approach with children whose classroom experience was largely with Scheme books.

As you can see I was unable to use 'apprenticeship' in a big way in my area but increasing numbers of schools were showing interest – and I also worked with a nursery school and play groups.
ANN NOSOWSKA

It will be clear that virtually all the experiences mentioned in this chapter have come from teachers of children with moderate learning difficulties or those in mainstream schools. I have had very little contact with teachers of children with severe difficulties in special schooling. I would very much like to have their view of the reading needs of their children. Are they too like the children from the Thomas Wolsey School in Ipswich whose staff visited my own school? This school caters for children from two years to nineteen with physical disabilities, many of whom have learning difficulties to a varying degree. The school uses a real-book, apprenticeship approach to their literacy learning. The pupils have books read to them, they share the reading, they read alone and they make their own books to read and share. In other words, they learn in just the same way as my class do.

All children are special; some have more needs than others. More needs – not different ones.

6 County Initiatives

So far, the apprenticeship approaches we have seen have been initiated at school level, in the classroom and staffroom, with the children and the teachers. And I feel very strongly that this is the best way for things to change. Especially these days, when so much of educational change is being imposed on schools without there being the heartfelt commitment that ensures success, it is one of the great strengths of most apprenticeship schools that they have changed because they want to, and because they believe in that change.

Alas, there have been some cases where county advisers or support teams have tried to impose change on schools that are less than convinced. I addressed this problem in the second edition of *Read with Me*, because I am concerned about it. Apprenticeship is no different from any other initiative in education: it cannot be successful in the hands of people who don't want to, or don't know how to, make it work.

However, several counties have put together wonderful support programmes for schools who want to begin apprenticeship approaches or who have begun and want help to continue. This chapter outlines a few of these initiatives. If you are lucky enough to live in any of these areas then you have a ready-made support system close at hand and easily available. If you live in other areas, that does not mean you have no similar support (I can only include those I know about), so do ask your language adviser or primary inspector. If there is nothing in your authority then hold up these examples of what can be done and press for improvement. It is unfortunate that too many advisers seem to view their job as requiring them only to go into schools, pat a few children on the head and say, 'Good, good' in an avuncular manner before departing back to the office to fill in some forms. (If you are an adviser, I'm sure there *is* more to it than that . . . but do teachers understand that?) Most teachers wish that advisers would support their teaching with more than smiles and nods. This chapter is intended to show what is being done by education authorities to support without coercion: a difficult balancing act but one that they manage amazingly well.

It was difficult to decide on the order in which I should introduce each authority and so, in traditional fashion (because we *do* teach the alphabet), they are included in alphabetical order.

The first initiative is from Brent, where the development of record-keeping, curriculum documents and policies has always taken place, within an overall framework of continuity of practice. Terry Furlong, the advisor for English and Drama, wrote to headteachers in Brent suggesting that language initiatives in the authority should be co-ordinated. This was both to ensure continuity throughout the borough and to make certain that the National Curriculum and its assessment procedures should be combined with what Brent schools saw as their view of the curriculum. The idea was to develop 'a coherent and intelligible system, common to all our schools in its main thrust, though varied to suit individual schools within its framework'. Suggesting that schools should join in this project, Terry summed up the need for sharing experience, problems and ideas in language policy by saying that the purpose of the development would be:

– to help learners become increasingly aware of their own progress;
– to involve parents in their children's learning and to inform them of their progress;
– to help teachers evaluate the effectiveness of their own teaching and planning;
– to help with early continuity within and between schools;
– to enable monitoring (by sampling) of educational standards both within the school and across the LEA.

Work could not begin in all areas simultaneously. Since a large number of schools throughout 86/87 and 87/88 have declared 'Language' to be their priority for GRIST and INSET activities including Baker Days and Directed Time, and many particular developments in record-keeping have grown out of this work, it seems a profitable, and indeed necessary, place to begin with this. Additionally, the Core Books project, bilingual instructors' initiative, Primary Language Post-Holders' Courses, Primary Humanities Guidelines, and a host of other contributions have helped to provide an essential preparation for these developments.

Further, an important aspect of any good record of achievement is the active involvement of parents and the children themselves. Parents already know a great deal about their children's development in language (and languages): it is a subject on which they can confidently contribute much information and insight on fairly equal terms with the school and its teachers. Also, it is an area of their learning about which it is possible for even quite young children to be fairly explicit and in which they can recognize their own achievements.   TERRY FURLONG

It is heartening to see a local authority proposing to involve parents directly in curriculum matters. This is often left to individual schools rather than being a deliberate part of the authorities' decision-making machinery.

Another authority working directly on home/school links and providing the school with support material to encourage and strengthen those links is Cleveland. For some years now a programme has supplied schools with materials to enable them to build up their home-reading links. The video they provide shows parents what shared reading is and how it works. The need felt by many schools for this kind of established-authority provision of information at initial parents' meetings is very great. I have spoken at many such meetings myself, and there is no doubt that some parents are very relieved to find out that apprenticeship is carried on successfully in other schools and has a history behind it. A video, of course, is also wonderful for demonstrating techniques like reading along with the child or sharing the reading.

The Cleveland video, 'Making Reading Fun', is available from Teesside Polytechnic Educational Development Unit, Borough Road, Middlesborough.

Dorset, too, supports parent/school reading projects with a comprehensive programme they have called 'Booked by Dorset'. I have had several tributes from Dorset's teachers to the help and inspiration this has been to them. It goes beyond exhortation or even demonstration, and involves the provision of resources such as books, tapes, games and storage materials. On pages 87-88 a report on 'Booked by Dorset' is reproduced from the January 1988 issue of *Signal*.

This sort of initiative seems to me to be ideal. It states the authority's belief in home/school links and the value of parental involvement in reading. It therefore sets the agenda. It does not force schools to take up any position against their will but provides support and resources for those schools who want to introduce or extend apprenticeship approaches. After all, even the most conventional school can make good use of a supply of new storybooks, language games or tapes, and the videos and booklets will enable such a school at least to know what the debate is about, even if it does not wish to join in.

A similarly global approach to support is provided by the Reading and Language Development Team in the London Borough of Haringey, where what I believe is an unusual approach to literacy support has been planned. It has a very full team of advisory teachers who are available to any school needing their presence. Unlike many advisory teachers these are
(continued on page 89)

Booked by Dorset

We invited Joan Hickmott, Primary Education Adviser in Dorset, to write about her county's encouragement of the 'real-book' approach to reading.

'Booked by Dorset' is one of the practical ways in which Dorset actively promotes the partnership between parents and teachers for the benefit of the children. From the beginning the scheme has been supported by the Chief Adviser, the Principal Schools' Officer and the County Library Service. It has been developed in the East and West of the county by two primary advisers with an early years' specialism. Before starting the scheme in 1984 we examined projects in other areas and then decided which particular approach we would like to take.

We thought it very important to acknowledge the fact that parents are the first and most influential teachers of their children. We wanted to establish the understanding of the complementary roles of parents and teachers and the value of working co-operatively, sharing information, expertise and experience to help the children to learn. We recognize that children start school with considerable experience of 'reading' and many have a good foundation for language development. They are, however, at different stages of development and understanding. 'Booked by Dorset' provides a natural framework for working together which increases the confidence and understanding of parents about ways in which they can help their child.

The Dorset project is based on the premise that children learn to read by reading, taking into account new insights about learning to read and the importance of language development. Above all, we want to ensure that reading is an enjoyable experience so that children are motivated to read for themselves, laying the foundations of an interest and pleasure for life. Through the project it is hoped to –

provide a range of books, games and activities through which parents and teachers can develop an interest in reading and language; give parents the opportunity to share in their own child's learning and give them a clearer picture of the ways in which children learn to read; provide a forum for a dialogue between parents and teachers regarding the motivation for and practice of reading; enable teachers to form closer links with parents; reduce the pressure on children by increasing the knowledge of the parents, encourage parents to work with their own child in school on a regular basis.

In much the same way that any project tries to establish an identity we agreed a name and designed a logo to be printed on carrier bags, bookmarks, link cards and booklets for parents and teachers. When a school joins the project, they are provided with: a selection of library books; taped stories and books with cassette recorders; a selection of language games and activities and hang-up bags for storage; video stories (these are a shared resource); booklets for teachers and parents; link cards; bookmarks; carrier bags for children to take books home; card for keeping records; letters for parents explaining the aim of the project and what is expected of them. The early planning of the project involved some psychologists and head teachers working with the advisers to produce the booklets and plan for monitoring and evaluation. The booklets have been revised since the start of the project, based on our experience.

In Dorset we have a wide range of school provision: very small rural schools; primary, infant and first schools; very large urban schools; schools receiving Urban Aid; schools on army bases; and clusters of small schools receiving an Education Support Grant. There is the normal disposition of parents who are articulate and have high expectations for their children and the schools alongside parents who are not as clear about their children's development and the role of the institution.

Schools usually initiate the discussions about becoming involved in 'Booked by Dorset', although sometimes the adviser may suggest it as a way of enhancing existing parental involvement in a school. The programme of preparation for a school wanting to join will include parent workshops to make games, organizing the space for parents to work with their children, arranging facilities for a crèche for the preschool children, and organizing the storage of materials. Teachers will be involved in some in-service, and they also visit other 'Booked by Dorset' schools.

The initial selection of books is made from a library supplier by teachers, advisers and a librarian; each school then chooses books from this selection to match their particular needs. The number of books varies with the size of the school, but there are usually about four books for each child involved. As the project moves up through a school, there is a top-up of books, and the county library replaces books that are lost or damaged. While most schools introduce the scheme for their youngest children, one or two have used it to boost the interest of seven-year-olds as the starting point in the school.

The two advisory teachers for the early years give the main support to the project. They assist with setting up the project, run workshops for parents and teachers, disseminate ideas for good practice and development, produce newsletters and a magazine, and run in-service sessions. The project started with nineteen schools in 1984; now nearly ninety schools participate, and there is a waiting list.

'Booked by Dorset' is funded mainly from the curriculum development fund, although other sources have been sought to extend the provision. When Dorset was awarded an Education Support Grant, £16,000 was included to bring all the rural schools involved into the scheme with a further £1600 annually to buy more books. Each of the two rural schools' projects has a preschool teacher who takes a fully equipped van into the villages and hamlets, lending books, games and activities to parents and giving advice about the learning development of their children. These children all start school where there is 'Booked by Dorset', and the parents are already used to working with their children through the Play and Learn vans. We are about to replicate this service in the far west of the county by bringing together Education, 'COMPACT', our Manpower Services Commission-funded project, and the Rural Development Agencies. COMPACT (community, parents and children and teachers) provides support for families with preschool children, encourages home/school links and gives help to 'Booked by Dorset'. Outreach workers take books and materials from school to homes, help provide crèche facilities, work with children if their parents are not able to come for a workshop, and generally help with the school sessions. There is also an outreach worker on the Play and Learn van to assist in keeping the records and helping with the toddlers while parents talk to the teacher. Not all schools can have the support of COMPACT, which only operates in parts of West Dorset, but they are tremendously helpful to the schools where they are attached.

We have not attempted to evaluate the scheme by means of testing, but schools monitor the attitudes towards reading of the parents and children. *All* the schools have very positive attitudes to the scheme even though it involves them in considerable extra work. Most schools have regular sessions for parents to work in school with their own child, but in some cases this has not been appropriate, especially where a high percentage of mothers are out at work. These schools encourage parental support at home, supported by meetings and some home visiting.

There are some eight thousand children in the scheme now with the preschool vans and our family centres and ninety schools. There has been an investment of about twelve pounds per child by the authority, with an immeasurable return for schools and families for that money.

not just there to pop in and out but are actually attached to the school, on request, and then work with the head, staff, children and parents for a year. This enables the school to plan, develop and implement a language programme with advice and cover.

Again this approach provides support without pressure (especially since schools have to request the team to involve themselves) and can be used whatever the present level of commitment to change. Details from the Reading and Language Development Team, High Cross Education Centre, Tottenham, London N17 6QP.

Another county that provides advisory teachers is Hertfordshire but here their role is slightly different. Two teachers, Chris Davis and Rosemary Stubbs, were seconded for a term to discover and respond to schools' needs for information and help in developing apprenticeship and shared reading projects. The outcome of this was a project which, like Dorset's scheme, provided stickers, books (at a wonderful discount!), parents' booklets and a video together with a booklet for teachers. This booklet, *Shared Reading: A Practical Guide for Teachers*, is one of the best outlines I have read of how schools, parents and books can come together to improve literacy. Again there is no hint of 'You must . . . ' about it. If a school wants to find out more about language policy development, there the information is, and there, also, are the resources and the help to enable the school to change with confidence and success.

Shared Reading: A Practical Guide for Teachers, (Education Department, Hertfordshire County Council, County Hall, Hertford SG13 8DF) describes the full project. In it the authors say:

. . . teachers are observing that children being taught in this way are showing more confidence in reading, a delight in story, and an ability to discriminate and amass information which has often been missing in the past. . . . There is no doubt that *Shared Reading* needs careful planning and monitoring, with extremely good lines of communication between teachers and parents. It needs a plentiful supply of books which must be changed frequently, because the children read so much more than they did before. But, once established, the advantages are infinitely worthwhile.

Teachers often tell me they feel isolated and alone when they want to make curriculum changes (and not only in language either). Very often they feel a lack of support, but even worse, a lack of interest and information. The number of teachers who, when I ask, don't know the name of their language adviser – or even if they've got one – is amazing and includes some headteachers as well. Others seem to see the advisory service's job as propping up failing schools or criticizing bad practice. The counties where the advisory service is most valued seem to be those whose advisers have a philosophy they believe in (what I might call 'preferred practice'): wanting to help schools to work towards that practice without forcing the pace, and providing the information and resources to enable them to do so. In other words, they have a coherent and cohesive view of what language teaching ought to be and how it should be developed.

So far we have covered only initiatives involved with beginning and sustaining apprenticeship programmes in schools. One authority went further, however. The Leicestershire Literacy Support Service began a project which they called 'Story Approach'. It originated several years ago as the means by which slow learners were enabled to begin again in literacy learning but, because of its success, was extended to include whole schools. A lovely booklet, *Once Upon a Time*, was produced for parents and teachers, outlining the thinking behind apprenticeship and explaining how it works. This was intended as a guide and a resource book for schools wanting to develop story approach. This booklet is available from the Leicestershire Literacy Support Service, Collegiate House, College Street, Leicester LE2 OJX.

In 1986, however, a new dimension was added with the start of the *Literacy Initiative Evaluation Project*. This study, by Muriel Bridge of the Literacy Support Service, of the developing reading behaviours of five-year-old pupils using 'traditional' methods or a 'story approach' evaluated the experiences of twenty-four Leicestershire primary or infant schools in beginning reading with reception children. The study initially involved 336 children and their teachers and the twenty-four schools were divided into twelve story-approach schools and twelve control schools who would be using a skills-based, reading-scheme approach. Preparations for the project included consultations with the English, Primary and Special Needs advisers and the library service.

A fully documented report (over 100 pages) on the project was published in Spring 1988. Its contents included descriptions of the background, aims and methods of the research and gave examples of headteachers' logs, class teachers' questionnaires, pupil interviews.

In Autumn 1988 another report was published which outlined the general findings and then studied in depth eighty-seven children in seven of the schools. The second-year evaluation came out at the end of 1988. The full report makes for fascinating reading, not only because of the light it sheds on the apprenticeship/traditional debate, but for the account of the way the study was undertaken. There are descriptions of the approaches to schools, the briefing for heads, the test circumstances and the teachers' and parents' reactions. In the summing-up:

Most reading behaviours of pilots ['story approach'] after two years are demonstrably more mature and independent than those of control ['traditional approach'] pupils.

What value, then, should be attached to measuring progress by standardised graded word tests, since all the behaviours noted above are 'hidden' beneath what appear to be similar standardised scores?

Are not later reading habits and reading competencies likely to be more positive and effective
- when children show at an early age a marked priority for and pleasure in sharing books
- when children make a search for meaning their first objective
- when children begin to develop a strategically integrated use of many positive reading cues?

Such early reading behaviours must surely give children a greater freedom and independence as readers who will be prepared not only to adapt their styles of reading to suit the text in hand, but who will always be ready to engage with and consult books as a prime source of information and enrichment.

After two years there are indications that a story approach may convince more young learners of the long-term value of reading and books. (Muriel Bridge in *Learning to Read: Literacy Initiative Evaluation Project, second year report, 1987-88*. A Study of the Developing Reading Behaviours of 5-year-old pupils using 'traditional' methods or a 'story approach'. Autumn 1988. Leicestershire Literacy Support Service, Collegiate House, College Street, Leicester LE2 0JX).

The notable thing about Leicestershire's work with 'story approach' is the amount of time and trouble taken by the Literacy Support Group to produce very high quality materials for schools. It is understandable that many authorities feel the need to keep costs down by photocopying and stapling but where a little more money has been made available, the finished product is very inviting.

In Shropshire some excellent booklets for teachers have been produced through the Shropshire Language Centre including studies of children's attitudes to books and the use of fiction and poetry in schools. These are made doubly interesting by the

(91)

mention of the actual books that can be used and by entertaining quotes from teachers and children, such as the child who said, 'I'm reading *David Copperfield*, because Mum says it's a Good Book. I think it's hard.' These booklets are available from Shropshire Language Centre, Hartsbridge Road, Oakengates, Telford, Salop. TF2 6BA.

One of the great pleasures in putting *Apprenticeship in Action* together has been the occasional exotic contact (such as the request to translate *Read with Me* into Danish, or to make of it a talking book for the blind). One such was the response from South Africa, which I have already mentioned in Chapter Three. The experience of Dr Lancaster in Pretoria, however, points to one important aspect of local authority initiatives. Dr Lancaster was intending to continue the project into the next three years in order to maintain support and monitoring over a length of time and with a large number of children. This seems to me something that needs to be considered more often. Schools are not served well if they are offered early support and encouragement which shifts to another priority in a year's time. The care over follow-up shown by Pretoria and, in England, Leicestershire is a model for all authorities providing initial support. It will also be noted that their interest covers the monitoring of progress, another important component of support that enables schools to assess what they are doing in a long-term, organized manner.

The project proved these strategies to be successful and we repeated, refined and extended the programme in 1987 and this year as well. We also continued with the original pupils in their second and third school years. We hope to continue for at least another three years (up to the 6th school year) in order to monitor their reading ability and their attitude towards reading. At the moment this project is running in twelve schools, with forty teachers and more or less 1000 pupils involved. The feedback is very positive.   M.M. LANCASTER

Some authorities are using individual schools as information centres for others. One such is Orchard House County Infant School in Warrington.

At the end of the Easter term, our head Mrs Perkin led an INSET meeting, organized by County Advisory Staff and held in our school, to show teachers from the county how we had approached and taken on board the apprenticeship reading. There were sixty visiting teachers who showed great enthusiasm for what we were doing. In fact throughout the county there is an increasing awareness of the value of apprenticeship reading.

Any students (teaching) who hear us say we don't use a reading scheme back us into corners and demand to know how it all works in the classroom.   BERYL WAINWRIGHT

This I find a very cheering idea. I like the sound of teachers doing the supporting and information-spreading; teachers do seem to take notice of other teachers. (The Colditz factor, I always think: only those in the prison camp know how to survive it!) School-based support programmes are more and more becoming a common way of using INSET money. The only problem is the burden it places on the host schools, so at this point perhaps I could offer some ground rules (from long personal experience) for schools wanting to visit other schools.

1. Don't expect to arrive tomorrow. Most 'show' schools are booked up a long way ahead (a term in our case). This is essential if the normal life of the school is to go on. Visitors take attention away from the children to an amazing extent and so have to be rationed to only one group every week at the very most. This is the cause of the waiting list.

2. Please don't expect to send more than four or five teachers at a time, especially to a small school. It is very tiring and overwhelming for a small staff to deal with swarms of people.

3. Please remember to confirm in writing, giving a contact phone number in case of need to cancel.

In return you will gain a great deal from a day spent in an apprenticeship school. There is nothing like spending time with people of a like philosophy to make you feel that you are not alone and that it is indeed possible and worthwhile after all.

Sometimes the support provided for schools is really the work of an individual within the county's structure. I had an interesting account of a project set up by Ann Nosowska when she was with her county's reading advisory service. She began a Family Reading Project which was intended particularly to support schools which admitted under-fives. It is also interesting because Ann started very much from where the schools were: not asking them to throw away all their familiar reading techniques but supporting them through a gradual change of approach.

I used this approach as a bridge from reading scheme to 'real' books in reception classes (4 + years in Warwickshire). It was based on the UKRA booklet *How to Run a Family Reading Group* by C. Obrist but I used it only with young children and their parents. As you know, schools are reluctant to change overnight chiefly because they may not have the funds and also because teachers feel more secure with a scheme. I see the Family Reading Project as a first step

(93)

in persuading teachers and parents.

It was initiated in the Spring of 1986 in a school where *One, Two, Three and Away* had recently been introduced (following 'Kathy and Mark'). The aim of the school initially is to use the apprenticeship approach for at least two terms before introducing the scheme books – but of course the apprenticeship approach is still used after that.

I obtained extra resources to put together a box of books - including 69 'real' books, and a set of Story Chest Stage 1. These books were used on a termly basis in schools in my area to involve parents and show them how apprenticeship works.

The procedure is as follows:

(a) Introductory meeting with parents.

(b) The reception child and his parent select a book (or books) to share at home.

(c) They return to school as a group – then subdivided into groups of six each week and show and talk about a book that they read together. After a few weeks some children are confident enough to talk on their own, to pseudo read or even read their chosen book. It is a useful way of ensuring that parents are following the correct approach too.

Those parents who want to can complete a record sheet and each child has a record card on which all the books borrowed are listed.

A video has been produced with the help of South Warwick College of Education and Bishopton Junior and Infant School to show stages of reading development using the apprenticeship approach. It is called START (Shared Time Actively Reading Together), which is shown to parents during the project.

The school where the Family Reading Group began now has parents calling in every morning at 9.00 a.m. to browse through the books with their children and the teachers continue the apprenticeship approach alongside the introduction of *One, Two, Three and Away*.

This is obviously only a half-way stage but it is quite an innovation!   ANN NOSOWSKA

Finally, I would like to turn to Wiltshire, where apprenticeship support is a matter of teamwork at its best. The impetus came initially from a group of schools; it was teacher-based and began as a mutual help group of the sort that many areas are setting up for themselves. The encouraging thing is the way the county support staff came in, together with initial and in-service trainers from Westminster College, to provide a team which had its feet firmly in the classroom but was supported by the county advisory teams. One of the teachers involved, Jan Maxwell, and Irene Suter from Westminster College tell the story of the project.

Once upon a time . . .

. . . there was an Infant Forum meeting held as part of Wiltshire's INSET programme, on a local basis. My deputy head and I were invited to talk to one of these meetings about our approach to reading. The meeting was entitled 'Reading without Schemes' and was attended by about fifty teachers.

Two things became clear from the discussion following our talk. Firstly that there was an enormous amount of interest in the approach and secondly that a number of people were already working without schemes (some having been doing so for a considerable time!).

There was, of course, a whole range of response but the overall impression was positive, with a number of teachers needing the assurance that someone was actually 'doing it' and that it *was* working.

It needs to be said that, at this stage, we ourselves were in the initial stages of using the approach and have developed the practicalities and the support activities considerably since then.

And then . . .

. . . In November 1986 a number of teachers were together at a meeting in Devizes to discuss children's writing, and during the coffee break the subject of the apprenticeship approach to reading cropped up. Jan Maxwell had introduced the subject when talking to the Infant Forum meeting mentioned above, and several of the Devizes group felt that a network of mutual support from teachers using 'the approach' could be helpful. The sole idea at that time was to enable such teachers to meet together to exchange ideas and discuss problems. Since Jan had first introduced the subject, and her own school had adopted the approach, it seemed natural to hold the first meeting at her school.

This meeting took place in March 1987. It was set up by word of mouth to people who we knew had a positive interest. One or two were unable to attend and so a select band of five met for a cup of tea and a chat. This included myself and my deputy Kathryn Nicholas (also an infant teacher), a member of our Area Support Team, another teaching head and a lecturer from Westminster College (Rene). It was clear even at this stage that sharing experiences, problems and worries was of great value and we felt that we would continue to meet and allow the group to grow like a ripple, by making personal contact with people and inviting them to join us. Little did we know! . . .

So it came about . . .

. . . that by using a personal-contact approach, we set up a second meeting at Christian Malford. The meeting was scheduled for 4

(95)

o'clock and we were expecting about fifteen colleagues. At 3.50 p.m. we were rushing about fetching more chairs, more cups and more biscuits! In fact, over thirty people turned up. Initially, to set the ball rolling, Jan and Kathryn talked about how they were working at their own school. They were supported by anecdotes from other teachers and a lively discussion followed.

However, it became obvious that, while there was a widespread and genuine interest in the ideas under discussion, the differences in knowledge and experience of the apprenticeship approach posed problems.

So it was decided to establish group meetings for different areas of the county and four group co-ordinators were appointed to organize them.

By hook or by crook . . .

. . . a pattern of meetings developed. The co-ordinators of the support groups which were set up in each area (Salisbury, Trowbridge, Swindon and Chippenham) circulated local schools inviting interested teachers to attend a meeting.

Here we made a vital mistake.

The aim was to discover how many teachers were using 'the approach' and to see how they would respond to the idea of regular meetings. However, we phrased the letter in a way that was ambiguous. We meant to address it to teachers who had already encountered the idea and were engaged in using it. What we discovered from the response was that there was a large number of people who wanted to know more about this new method of 'teaching reading', and we were absolutely swamped with replies. However, the meetings went ahead, each attended by 50-60 people and we did our best.

The meetings were composed of some people who had read *Read with Me*, understood that it was a philosophical approach rather than another 'method' and in some cases were already trying it for themselves, and many others who were interested, but had not ever known about the booklet.

O'er hill and dale . . .

. . . Rene or I went to each meeting, talked about the apprenticeship approach, answered questions and chatted informally.

From this beginning each group has developed in its own way with its own strengths and/or problems. One group is strong, fairly large and therefore fairly structured, one is fairly small and informal, one has ceased to function, one fluctuates and a new one has just been formed. What is clear, however, from those groups that are operating is the benefit of being able to share experiences, talk over problems and sort out ideas.

Common factors which everyone seems to want to discuss include parents (how to convince them), record-keeping, which books work, ethnic minorities, being a 'loner' on the staff, and the crucial part played by the books themselves and the consequent need for teachers to extend their own book knowledge.

As far as county developments are concerned, we held a meeting at school for people interested in the apprenticeship approach in March and four people attended. We held a follow-up meeting in June and over thirty came. Consequently we have set up four area support groups, circulated all the schools in the county and have been flooded with replies. It remains to be seen where we go from here.   JAN MAXWELL & IRENE SUTER

The most cheering thing about these local authority initiatives is the extent to which they are seen as providing support and information without coercion. Where resources are also offered, as in Hertfordshire's cheap book purchase scheme, all schools can benefit, and those wanting change have a potential discouragement removed. If the project includes some form of follow-up, change will be taking place in an atmosphere of care and responsibility – as it must to be successful and long-term.

7   Summing Up . . .

I want to finish *Apprenticeship in Action* with two letters. The first
is from Niki Stanley, an American teacher who has spent two
years working in Oxford. She wrote to describe to me the path
she travelled as she introduced apprenticeship reading to her
class in the United States. There is as much learning for the
teacher as for the children.

As a 'teacher of reading' with nine- and ten-year olds I felt that the
basal reader [reading scheme] method of teaching lacked
something. It was uninteresting and lacklustre to me, and I figured
my students must feel the same way. Furthermore, if I followed all
the suggestions in the teacher's manual the children would read one
story a week and fill the rest of their reading time with poorly
designed worksheets and workbooks. Apart from daily silent
reading the children had little involvement in actual reading. For
many years I have included time for silent reading and read–aloud
sessions. Yet I felt that there was more that could be done to spark
interest and make real readers of my students. So I embarked on a
plan to eliminate gradually the use of the basal reader and get
children more involved with books. Why not use children's novels
instead of short stories that some publishing company chose for me
to use?
   I decided to start with the most able readers because I felt that
they were good enough to live through my mistakes(!) while I
learned what worked best. I made my start by choosing a book
which I knew to be popular with children and that I enjoyed as
well. I obtained enough copies for all the children in that group. I
assigned an amount to be read for discussion, I occasionally gave
questions or small projects related to the assignment, and we met
together to discuss what we read. In that way we were able to
discover together various elements of text that we might not have
if each child had read the selection alone. The children became
more interested in their reading, they learned more from what they
read, they became more mature readers, they learned to discuss
ideas with each other, and together we began to have a new
appreciation for literature in general.
   As I matured in this new approach, I began to work with the
other children in the same way, according to their abilities, until I
had eliminated the use of the basal [scheme] altogether. This took

several years. I worked with children in groups that I formed, I let them form their own groups according to their own interest in books which were available, and there were times when the children were reading individual books of their choice. Sometimes the groups were reading books which were all related in some way – theme, genre, etc. – and related to what I was reading aloud to them. Then we discussed as a class the similarities and differences in the books to gain a broader understanding of that particular type of literature.

At this time I also involved the children and myself in more writing. As a result I gained a better understanding of the connection between reading and writing. I really began to see terrific things happen with the children when they made that connection. I use journals instead of worksheets and workbooks, and I encourage children to respond in writing to what they are reading, not only with reading as a subject, but in all areas of the curriculum. Consequently, the children have grown from writing 'I liked this story because it was nice (or had lots of action)' to putting some real thought into what they write, thinking about how it made them feel, what kind of reaction they had, what it reminded them of, whether it was like any other story they'd ever read, what seemed realistic, what made it fantasy and why, etc. I respond in writing to their journal entries whenever possible.

I have used all sorts of 'devices' to get my students reading. As a result I rarely have a child in my class who does not enjoy reading. I have a large collection of books for our classroom library categorized by genre for easier access. I talk about the books in the room and let them know when a new book has been added to the collection. We talk about book awards such as Newbery, Caldecott, Carnegie, Greenaway, etc.; spend time talking about authors and illustrators; look at birthdays of those people and read related books. I give the children a time to have shared reading with each other and to tell the class about a book they have read that they may want to recommend. I introduce them to all kinds of poetry, regularly adding poems to their poetry folders. We have a poem of the month. We work on memorizing poetry by reading the monthly poem together almost every day so that most of the children have memorized it by the end of the month. I bring in books from the public library for pleasure reading and for use in science and social studies.

I enjoy reading and try to make it as exciting to the children as possible. It's imperative that I read something during silent reading times so that they see me reading for pleasure – a sort of 'practise what you preach'. I try to stay informed about what's published in the field of children's literature so that I can expose my students to high quality literature.

Since I have changed my philosophy about reading, based on research on how children learn, my students have an enthusiasm for reading that would never have been achieved with the traditional method I started with. I have personally discovered that children become readers by reading, and I provide many opportunities for them to do so.   NIKI STANLEY

The second letter expresses so well the experiences enjoyed by so many of the teachers in this collection that I immediately wanted to use it to sum up the feelings of all of us. I then lost the covering letter! As a result this wonderful description of a teacher's philosophy is appearing anonymously in the first edition of *Apprenticeship in Action*, and I can only beg the writer of the following letter to get in touch with me again so that I can give proper credit for it. So, with many apologies to my correspondent for my carelessness, here is *Learning about Learning to Read*.

Seventeen years ago, the process of learning to read was illuminated for me by a five-year-old. Very few experiences, professional or personal, are so clearly imprinted on my mind.

Michael was an ordinary little boy of average intelligence who preferred sand, water, and bricks to books. I thought perhaps if he spent the obligatory five minutes (or was it three?) 'reading to me' at lunchtime, when the other 38 children were in the playground, we might make some progress. Oblivious to his view of this procedure (since it was no punishment to me) I asked him to stay behind and fetch his 'reading' book. Stoically, he obliged, and stood beside my desk with an early 'Janet and John' book. He had struggled to about page ten of this epic tale – the text was 'Look John, see the boats'. After studying the picture solemnly for a few moments, he said, 'Look John, the boat's stuck. Let's go and get a stick.'

Picture, if you can, the tumult of emotions into which I was thrown! Helplessness, at my own lack of knowledge, for my training hadn't prepared me for this. Frustration, at the sheer inadequacy of the 'Reading Scheme'. Above all, admiration and respect for the child, untrammelled as yet by classroom conventions, and still trying to bring his own sense of fun and normal life to this book. For it was a book – though it certainly wasn't what Michael was looking for – a story!

I was just out of my probationary year, with 39 children on roll, ages from five to seven. Many would have said then, and some would still say, that I should have made sure that Michael 'knew' the five words on that page before going to the even more tedious and unmemorable words on page eleven. To my eternal relief, intuition got in the way. I told him that I liked his story much better than the one in the book – then read him the printed text, pointing out the words, and soon afterwards he escaped, relatively unscathed, to join his friends in the playground.

I cannot pretend that Michael became a fluent reader overnight. If I had known then what I know now, if there had been better books, smaller classes, and parent helpers, perhaps we would have done better. At least I feel confident that he did not develop a sense of failure and inadequacy at my hands.

This probably seems a pitifully small achievement, but there are, even now, classrooms where children gain only a sense of failure and inadequacy, particularly in relation to reading.

This is very seldom because teachers are lazy, incompetent, or unkind. On the contrary, some of the most hard-working, well-organized and best-intentioned of teachers still create the situations which lead children to say 'I'm not very good at reading' at the age of six or seven.

Seventeen years ago, I was given the chance to listen to and learn from the children in my care. I read, attended courses, and discussed curriculum matters with colleagues. But it was always from the children that I learned most. I learned that reading is learned, not taught, and that children learn to read by reading.

They do not learn to talk, walk, swim, or ride a bike by being told how to, but by doing these things. To say this is in no way to lessen the role of the teacher. On the contrary, knowing when and how to offer guidance and explanation can develop and refine all these skills immeasurably. So with reading, sensitive and appropriate intervention (or non-intervention) is all important.

Later in my career I met James. He was twelve, had been categorized as a slow learner, and placed in a special school. His vision and hearing were impaired, he suffered from epilepsy, and, when we met, was unable to recognize any words except his name. He was an emotional, affectionate boy, whose moods swung from joyous enthusiasm to black despair.

We made books together about the things which interested him, and read them together over and over again, until he wanted a new one. When he *chose* to bring me books from another well-known reading scheme, we shared those. We looked at the shapes of individual words and letters from time to time; always, though, within context which he saw as meaningful and relevant. By the age of thirteen, he could read like an average seven-year-old, his self-esteem soared and he was confident to tackle anything he chose. He also went, in this time, from producing the equivalent of two-year-old scribble, to writing legible infant script.

I was still learning! In my next school, children had access to several reading schemes. Sadly, these were often used as further hurdles for the children rather than as a broadening experience. I started to introduce Puffins, and anything else I could beg or borrow, to my rising eight-year-olds, not as carrots for the better readers who had 'finished' the reading scheme, but for all of the children to choose whenever they wished. I did this tentatively at first, but more and more confidently as the children responded with pleasure to read real books and stories. I gradually learned to give 'real' freedom, not to expect every book to be completed, or every page to be read to me, but was still trying to hear every child read aloud daily. I attended courses on miscue analysis, I read Frank Smith, and others, and I went on listening to the children, and finding out what helped them to learn.

The school was in the middle of a high rise council estate in a rather bleak suburb, with the nearest book shop a bus ride away, and even the public library across a major dual carriageway! I was the main source of books for most of the children. Some of my colleagues viewed my approach with anxiety, but my children were, by this time, reading a range of traditional and modern children's prose and poetry which spoke for itself, and needed little justification. What's more, they were devouring them eagerly, talking to each other and to me about them, asking to be next with certain well-thumbed favourites, and asking to read them again. The books I had read as class stories were often in great demand, as were those which were dramatized on television.

Perhaps that was when I should have undertaken further study? I did – in mathematical education 5-13!

By the time I moved to my next school as deputy head, I knew that most children could learn to read with any books, or no books. I also knew that, for me, to return to the stultifying world of the reading scheme would be like putting children in a darkened room when outside the sun was shining on a garden.

Were there no children who failed to respond to this approach? Am I painting an altogether too rosy picture? In the last ten years, I can recall only one child of eight who went on to middle school effectively a non-reader. Many were fluent, voracious, committed readers. Several saw themselves as failing at seven, and underwent a transformation in terms of self-esteem and confidence by eight.

I know of none who disliked books and stories, didn't want to read, or felt that they couldn't read. By treating all the children as apprentice readers from the beginning, we are learning together all the time, and too busy enjoying the books to count whether we know more words than the next person, or are reading 'harder' books.

For every child who does not succeed in learning to read with 'real books', I guarantee you'll find at least one disillusioned non-reader struggling through a reading scheme where used. This way, however, the door is left open into the garden, and no one feels they have to stay in the dark.

Now that I have overall responsibility for the curriculum, including language, my aim is to see that all of the children in my care have the opportunity, not just to learn to read, but to learn to read with pleasure and confidence, and to develop the beginnings of a lifelong love of books.

My colleagues are all lively, thinking people. Some of them have whole-heartedly embraced the move away from reading schemes. Even those who are a little anxious about it have shown an abundance of goodwill. In particular, I have both an outstanding deputy, and a very enthusiastic language co-ordinator.

I am confident that we can gradually build up our 'real book' resources, although the size of the initial outlay has been quite alarming, and we have a long way to go. We managed to obtain a grant for books emphasizing the multicultural aspects of our society from a charitable trust, and the children's library service has been supportive, promising to upgrade our stock of non-fiction. This will release more funds for good stories and poetry.

I have, I know, the support and goodwill of the advisory service, who will give whatever help they are able.

Parents are welcomed into the school in a number of capacities. There is a parent-teacher language initiative called 'Booked by Dorset', in which parents undertake project work with their own child, and sometimes others. We welcome parents' help about the school in many ways, and have also invited them to meetings at which the move away from reading schemes, and the reasons behind it, have been explained.

There is still, however, a minority of parents who are expressing vociferous alarm. Indeed, I have been quite surprised to discover the extent to which the reading scheme has become one of the 'pillars of society' – or at least of recognizable and safe education in the eyes of many parents. It is a sad reflection on that society when any set of books, published and written by anyone, illustrated anyhow, and containing any nonsense under the sun, so long as it is labelled a 'READING SCHEME', is seen as more valuable than the knowledge and experience of teachers. I have been, as usual, too lacking in guile – obviously I should have told parents that all the wonderful new books and stories we have obtained recently, are our new 'READING SCHEME'!

One of the most important things about this letter is its title. All the contributors to *Apprenticeship in Action* share a belief in the necessity to continue learning about what readers do and need. It is, if you like, the very opposite of the publishers' model of the teaching process, which prescribes and proscribes with

(103)

perfect confidence exactly what the teacher and child shall do. It seems to me that the teachers who have written to me (and the initial contact was always theirs) are those who most feel that neither they nor their children could be fitted into and follow the prescribed course. They are willing to think about and question assumptions and to look, not at what the children ought to be doing, but at what they actually *are* doing. It is this willingness to learn from children that characterizes all those who wrote to me and is so well expressed by the teacher of Michael and James.

One more point remains. Most of this book has been concerned with organization and teaching practice. It may have given the impression that the child learning to read is a product only of parents' meetings, book display, reading records and the colour of the book markers: that the product of teaching reading is the ability to read. This is, of course, not true. The medium by which children learn to read is literature, not organization, and the proof of that learning is the love of reading.

In short, there has been far too little mention of books in these pages. Readers of *Read with Me* will know how firmly I believe that books are not just the means by which children learn – they are the purpose of the learning – and that the books themselves do the teaching for us. Only by offering high-quality books that children love will the real business of learning take place. Says Sylvia Ashton Warner, 'A five [year old] meeting words for the first time and finding they have intense meaning for him, at once loves reading. And this is the . . . issue. Love of reading. Love of books . . . which brings me back to the consideration of reading books as an integral factor in a child's life.'

It is not the way books are organized or recorded that will make the child a true reader; it is the intense meaning the words hold. We cannot organize the intensity and the meaning, or record them in attainment targets or key stages. They are too personal. As long as we remember this, we will keep a proper sense of our place, and the place of the National Curriculum, in a child's life. It is the books that are integral to the child. We are only the providers of the opportunity to read them.